Jazzy Pots

GLORIOUS GIFT IDEAS

Jazzy Pots

GLORIOUS GIFT IDEAS

Mickey Baskett

Sterling Publishing Co., Inc.
New York

Prolific Impressions Production Staff:

Editor in Chief: Mickey Baskett
Copy Editor: Phyllis Mueller
Graphics: Dianne Miller, Karen Turpin
Styling: Kirsten Jones
Photography: Jerry Mucklow, Joel Tressler
Administration: Jim Baskett

Every effort has been made to insure that the information presented is accurate. Since we have no control over physical conditions, individual skills, or chosen tools and products, the publisher disclaims any liability for injuries, losses, untoward results, or any other damages which may result from the use of the information in this book. Thoroughly read the instructions for all products used to complete the projects in this book, paying particular attention to all cautions and warnings shown for that product to ensure their proper and safe use.

Library of Congress Cataloging-in-Publication Data Available

10 9 8 7 6 5 4 3 2

Published by Sterling Publishing Co., Inc.
387 Park Avenue South, New York, N.Y. 10016

© 2004 by Prolific Impressions, Inc.

Produced by Prolific Impressions, Inc.
160 South Candler St., Decatur, GA 30030

Distributed in Canada by Sterling Publishing
c/o Canadian Manda Group, One Atlantic Avenue, Suite 105
Toronto, Ontario, Canada M6K 3E7
Distributed in Great Britain by Chrysalis Books Groups PLC
The Chrysalis Building, Bramley Road, London W10 6SP, England
Distributed in Australia by Capricorn Link (Australia) Pty. Ltd.
P.O. Box 704, Windsor, NSW 2756 Australia

Acknowledgements

Thanks to the following suppliers for providing materials for creating these jazzy pots:

Art Accents *for Postalz™ flower postage stamps*;
Environmental Technologies Inc., www.eti-use.com *for two-part pour-on resin*;
Lazertran, www.lazertran.com, *for transfer film*;
Plaid Enterprises, Norcross, GA 30092, (800)392-8673, www.plaidonline.com, *for FolkArt® Acrylic Colors, FolkArt® Artists' Pigments™, FolkArt® Sparkles, Paint for Plastic, Durable Colors indoor/outdoor gloss enamels, Stencil Decor® stencils and stenciling supplies, FolkArt® sealers and varnishes.*

CONTENTS

Clay flower pots — those useful, inexpensive, widely available containers — are versatile surfaces for decorating that can assume a variety of guises. In this book, you'll find pots used as garden ornaments, birdbaths and feeders, fountains, tableware and table bases, gift packaging, storage and, of course, planters.

POTS GALORE
FOR
GLORIOUS GIFT GIVING

This book showcases the work of an array of talented designers who've put their minds and hands to making creative decorated pots for a variety of uses. There are more than three dozen projects — each with easy to follow step-by-step instructions, plus patterns, worksheets, painting examples, and assembly diagrams.

Some projects are simple, some are ornate. Some involve one pot, some a whole stack. The techniques include design painting, decoupage, stamping, sponging, stenciling, crackling, combing, and decorating with polymer clay, glass, shells, and buttons. You'll find something for everyone on your gift list, and a few you'll want to give to yourself. Enjoy!

Pot Decorating Supplies
PAINT

Painting a clay pot is one of the easiest and quickest ways to transform your plain clay pot into a work of art or whimsy. Be sure to choose the right kind of paint for the job.

■ Acrylic Craft Paint

You will be able to find a wide variety of colors of these paints that are made especially for decorative painting. They are available in convenient plastic squeeze bottles. Acrylic craft paints are richly pigmented, flat finish paints that come ready to use. They are available in a huge range of pre-mixed colors, including rich metallics, glitters, and sparkles. Use these types of paint as base paints to completely cover your pot or to do design painting. This type of paint is not resistant to the elements, so if you are going to use your pot outdoors, you will need to make sure it is adequately sealed after the paint is dry.

■ Tube Acrylics

Artist tube acrylics can also be used to paint designs on your pot. They are thick and need to be mixed with water or a medium to bring them to a painting consistency. When using these paints, your project will need to be adequately sealed if using the pot outdoors.

■ Indoor/Outdoor Gloss Enamels

Indoor/outdoor gloss enamels are weather-resistant and durable. They dry to a glossy sheen and can be used outdoors without a protective finish. These paints usually are available in a limited color range as compared to the regular acrylic craft paints.

■ Bakeable Enamel Paint

Bakeable enamels are acrylic paints that can be baked in a home oven to create a finish that is washable and top-rack dishwasher-safe. They provide opaque coverage and dry to a glossy sheen. Some brands of this type of paint can also be air cured, others have to be baked to make them permanent. Be sure to read the instructions on the label for use and curing the paint.

FINISHES

To protect your painted pot project, you will need to coat your painting with some type of protective varnish or sealer. There is a wide range of sealers available. Be sure they are compatible with the paint you are using and will provide adequate protection for the area where you are using your pot.

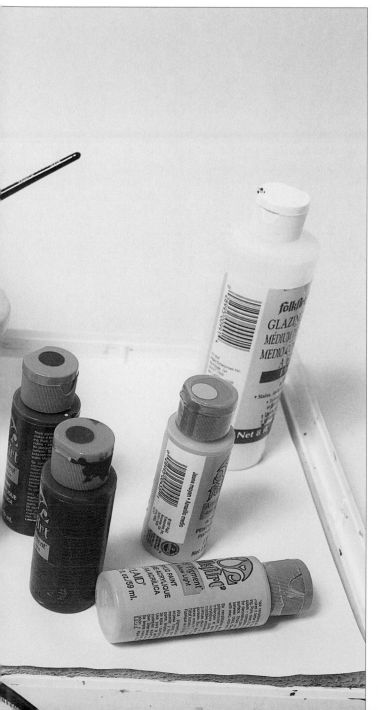

◾ Clear Acrylic Aerosol Finishes

Aerosol finishes are clear-drying spray-on coatings that protect surfaces from moisture and dust. They are available in flat, satin, and gloss sheens. For best results, use several thin coats rather than one thick one. If using your pot outdoors, be sure you purchase a finish rated for outdoors.

◾ Brush-on Waterbase Finishes

Brush-on waterbase finishes (often called waterbase varnishes) are quick-drying, clear finishes you apply with a brush. They are available in a variety of sheens.

◾ Brush-on Outdoor Varnish or Sealers

Outdoor sealers are specifically designed for sealing and protecting surfaces that will be used outdoors. They are polyurethane based and clear-drying.

◾ Two-Part Resin Finish

This type of finish will create a very thick, shiny, and durable finish. The two parts of the finish are mixed together, then the finish is poured over the pot.

◾ Decoupage Finish

Decoupage finish can be used for not only gluing paper designs to your pot, but also can be used to coat the pot for protection. This type of finish is not recommended if you are planning to use your pot outside or if it is going to come in contact with liquids or wet items.

BRUSHES & APPLICATORS

■ Artist's Paint Brushes

Artist's paint brushes – flats, rounds, and liners – are used for painting designs on pots and for lettering. Experienced painters recommend you use the best brushes you can afford and clean and care for them meticulously so they will last. Two good guidelines for choosing brushes are to use the size brush that fits the design and feels comfortable to you.

■ Foam (or Sponge) Brushes

Foam brushes are handy for base painting and for applying crackle medium, decoupage finish, varnish or glue.

■ Varnish Brushes

Varnish brushes are short-bristle brushes used for applying varnish. They come in a variety of widths.

■ Sponges

Sponges are useful for applying paint to create textures and designs. Compressed sponges, which you buy dry and flat, can be cut into shapes with scissors and hydrated to make sponge shapes for stamping.

A variety of quality artist brushes for painting your designs.

Preparing Pots

SURFACE PREPARATION

1. Wash pots with vinegar and water to remove any dirt or oils. Scrub them with a brush if necessary. Let pots air dry completely.
2. If holes need to be drilled in the pot, use a carbide masonry drill bit. Make the holes *before painting*, in case the pot or saucer gets broken or develops a crack during drilling.
3. Paint the project according to the individual project instructions.
4. When paint is dry, apply the varnish of your choice to protect the painting.

TRANSFERRING PATTERNS

The patterns for the projects that require them are located on adjacent pages to the project. Follow this procedure to transfer a pattern to your pot:

1. Trace the pattern from the book onto **tracing paper**. Enlarge or reduce, if necessary on a photocopier so the design fits your intended pot.
2. Position the traced pattern on your project. Slip **transfer paper**, shiny side down, between the project and the traced pattern.
3. Re-trace the pattern lines *lightly* with a **stylus** to transfer the design.

SOME CAUTIONS

- If you plan to use the pot for planting or placing any type of wet substance inside it, we recommend you seal the inside of your pot with an outdoor varnish or a two-part resin sealer. Pots are very porous and liquid inside the pot will migrate through the pot to the outside. As a result your decoration might be damaged if the inside is not sealed.

- *Do not* paint the insides of pots if you plan to plant live plants directly in the pot. That said, we recommend you *not* plant directly in the pot. For best results, and to preserve your painting, place another pot inside your painted pot to hold plants.

- If using pots to present or store food, *do not* allow the food to come into contact with a painted surface. Use plastic liners, glass containers, or plastic bags to contain foods if the pot is painted on the inside. (It's okay for food to contact a clean, unpainted clay surface.)

FAUX MOSAIC SAUCER

A large clay saucer is a versatile container with many uses. Here, it's used as a base for holding candles. It can also make a great tray or platter to use outdoors (or indoors). If you paint it with bakeable enamel paint, you can wash it – but don't let food touch the paint. For serving, use a clear glass plate on top of the saucer to hold food.

SUPPLIES

Surface:

Clay saucer, 12" diameter

Paints:

Enamel paint

    Cobalt Blue

    Engine Red

    Fresh Foliage Green

    Hydrangea Blue

    Licorice Black

    Pure Orange

    Sunflower Yellow

Tools & Other Supplies:

Compressed sponge

1/4" diameter wooden dowel, cut into seven 4" lengths (optional)

Glue

Craft knife

Palette or disposable plates

Painter's masking tape

Pencil

INSTRUCTIONS

Supplies

Stamping the design.

Make Sponge Stamps:
1. Cut seven squares from the compressed sponge, each 1/2" (one for each color of paint).
2. Dip squares in water to reconstitute. Allow to dry thoroughly.
3. *Optional:* To make the sponge squares easier to use, glue each sponge square to the end of a piece of wooden dowel. Let dry.

Create the Faux Mosaic Design:
1. Make sure saucer is clean and dry.
2. Use a pencil to mark off stripes of various widths across the saucer.
3. Place painter's tape on sides of saucer to protect the area from paint.
4. Place puddles of all paint colors on palette (or plate), allowing enough space around puddles to work paint into sponge squares.
5. Load one square stamp with paint by pouncing along the edge of the paint puddle. Pounce loaded stamp on a clean area of the palette to remove excess paint and to work the paint into the stamp.
6. Press the stamp on the saucer to make tile-like impressions. Fill each stripe with stamped squares of paint, leaving a small amount of space between each stamped square. Use masking tape as needed to protect areas from paint. You can usually get several stampings from your sponge square before you have to reload with paint.
7. Load another stamp with next color and repeat the stamping process until desired area is filled with squares of paint.
8. Allow paint to cure or bake in a home oven according to the instructions on the label for the brand of paint you have chosen.

To use: Hand wash saucer or wash on the top rack of your dishwasher.

Caution! Do not allow food to touch the painted surface. ❑

FAUX MOSAIC POTS

SUPPLIES

Pots:

Clay pots, 8" and 10" diameter

Paints:

Enamel paint - 3 to 5 colors of your choice

Tools & Other Supplies:

Compressed sponge

1/4" diameter wooden dowel, cut into seven 4" lengths

Glue

Craft knife

Palette or disposable plates

Painter's masking tape

INSTRUCTIONS

Make Sponge Stamps:

1. Cut seven squares from the compressed sponge, each 1/2" (one for each color of paint).
2. Dip squares in water to reconstitute. Allow to dry thoroughly.
3. Glue each sponge square to the end of a piece of wooden dowel. Let dry.

Create the Faux Mosaic Design:

1. Make sure rim of pot is clean and dry.
2. Place painter's tape on sides of pot under rim to protect area from paint.
3. Place puddles of all paint colors on palette (or plate), allowing enough space around puddles to work paint into the sponge squares.
4. Load one square stamp with paint by pouncing along the edge of the paint puddle. Pounce loaded stamp on a clean area of the palette to remove excess paint and to work the paint into the stamp.
5. Press the stamp on the pot to make tile-like impressions. Leave a small amount of space between each stamped square. Use masking tape as needed to protect areas from paint.
6. Load another stamp with next color and repeat the stamping process until the rim is filled with squares of paint. Change colors as desired to create the design of your choice.
7. To be sure paint is permanent and washable, allow paint to cure according to the instructions on the label for the brand of paint you have chosen. ❏

CHIC CLAY TABLE

By Kirsten Jones

A large painted clay pot can make an interesting table base.
The glass top reveals the crackled interior.

SUPPLIES

Pot:

Standard clay pot, 17" *or a size you choose to be your table base.*

Paints, Mediums & Finishes:

Acrylic craft paints

    Fresh Foliage

    Licorice

Crackle medium

Outdoor varnish - satin

Tools & Other Supplies:

1" flat brush

Painter's masking tape

20" round glass top

INSTRUCTIONS

1. Paint inside and outside of pot with Licorice, Let dry.

2. Following manufacturer's instructions, apply crackle medium to entire inside of clay pot. Let dry.

3. Brush over crackle medium with Fresh Foliage. Cracks will form. Let dry.

4. Apply painter's tape to outside of pot, creating stripes 1-1/2" wide.

5. Paint stripes with Fresh Foliage. You will need a thick paint coverage or several coats of paint so that the black will not show through. Let dry. Remove tape.

6. Seal with outdoor varnish. Let dry.

7. Place the glass top on the pot to create the table. ❑

PICNIC POTS

By Holly Buttimer

Decorated pots make great containers for outdoor dining, especially when they are painted with garden motifs. Use them to hold napkins or utensils. Or fill a tin bucket with ice, place the bucket in a pot, and use it to keep beverages chilled. When fitted with plastic or other food-safe liners, painted pots can be serving pieces for fruit or snacks. You can also paint other containers, like trays or plates or saucers, to coordinate with your painted pots.

Bug Pot

Pattern on page 22

SUPPLIES

Pot:

Standard clay pot, 10"

Paints & Finishes:

Acrylic craft paints

(see color chart)

Clear acrylic aerosol sealer

Tools & Other Supplies:

Paint combing tool *or* graining tool

Glazing medium

Tracing paper and pencil

Transfer pencil and stylus

Artist brushes

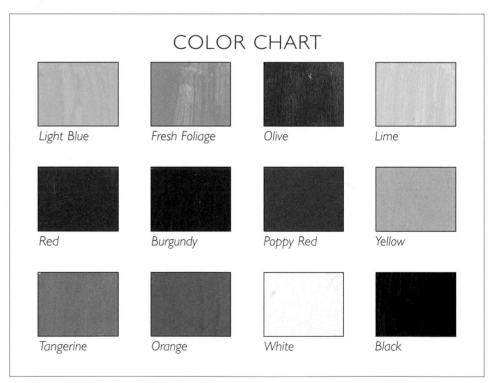

COLOR CHART

Light Blue	*Fresh Foliage*	*Olive*	*Lime*
Red	*Burgundy*	*Poppy Red*	*Yellow*
Tangerine	*Orange*	*White*	*Black*

INSTRUCTIONS

Base Paint:

1. Base paint pot with Light Blue. Paint rim with lime. Let dry.
2. Mix Olive paint 50/50 with glazing medium. Brush Olive paint mixture over the rim. While the paint is still wet, remove some of the paint with a combing or graining tool to create texture. Let dry.
3. Trace and transfer the design.

Paint the Orange Butterfly:

1. Paint wings with Orange.
2. Highlight with Yellow, Tangerine, and White.

Continued on page 22

Tulip Pot

Pictured on page 19

Pattern on page 23

SUPPLIES

Pot:

Standard clay pot, size 8"

Paints & Finishes:

Acrylic craft paints

  (see color chart)

Clear acrylic sealer

Tools & Other Supplies:

Paint combing tool

Glazing medium

Tracing paper and pencil

Transfer pencil and stylus

Artist brushes

INSTRUCTIONS

Base Paint:

1. Base paint pot with Light Blue. Paint rim with lime. Let dry.
2. Mix Olive paint 50/50 with glazing medium. Brush Olive paint mixture over the rim. While the paint is still wet, remove some of the paint with a paint comb to create texture.
3. Trace and transfer the design.

Paint the Tulips:

1. Paint petals with Poppy Red, Magenta, Crimson, and Orange.
2. Shade with Burgundy.
3. Highlight with Yellow and White.

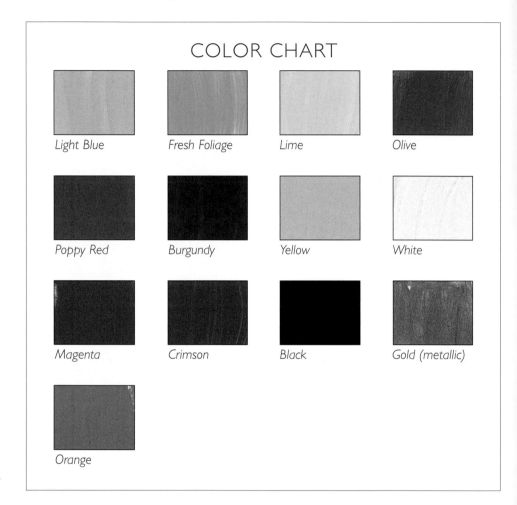

COLOR CHART

Light Blue   Fresh Foliage   Lime   Olive

Poppy Red   Burgundy   Yellow   White

Magenta   Crimson   Black   Gold (metallic)

Orange

Paint the Leaves:

1. Paint leaves with Fresh Foliage.
2. Highlight with Lime.
3. Shade with Olive.

Paint the Butterfly:

1. Paint wings with Orange.
2. Highlight with Yellow, and White.
3. Shade with Poppy Red and Burgundy.
4. Add details with Black.
5. Paint body with Black. Add White

highlights.

Paint the Bee:

1. Paint body with Black and Yellow. Paint wings with White.
2. Highlight body with White. Shade with Gold. Let dry.

Finish:

Seal with acrylic sealer. Let dry. ❏

CHERRY TRAY

By Holly Buttimer

Pictured on page 19
Pattern on page 24

SUPPLIES

Surface:

Wooden tray with rim and rounded corners, approx. 10" x 14"

Paints & Finishes:

Acrylic craft paints
  (see color chart)

Clear acrylic sealer

Tools & Other Supplies:

Sea sponge

Transfer paper and stylus

Tracing paper and pencil

Sandpaper

Tack cloth

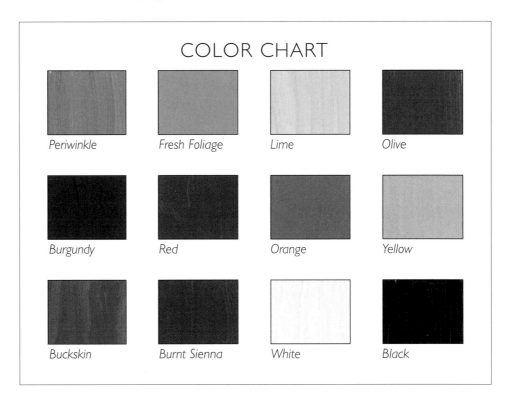

COLOR CHART

Periwinkle	Fresh Foliage	Lime	Olive
Burgundy	Red	Orange	Yellow
Buckskin	Burnt Sienna	White	Black

INSTRUCTIONS

Base Paint:

1. Sand tray. Wipe away dust. Mark off the border on the inside of the tray.
2. Paint inside the border with Lime.
3. Paint border with Periwinkle. Paint outside of tray with Periwinkle.
4. Sponge outside of tray with Lime.
5. Paint rim with White.
6. Paint checks on rim with Black.
7. Paint wavy line on border with Lime. Add dots to border with Black. Let dry.

8. Trace and transfer the design.

Paint the Design:

1. Paint cherries with Red. Highlight with Orange and White. Shade with Burgundy.
2. Paint stems with Buckskin. Shade with Burnt Sienna. Highlight with White.
3. Paint leaves with Fresh Foliage. Highlight with Lime. Shade with Olive.
4. Paint butterfly's wings with Orange. Shade with Burgundy. Highlight with Yellow and White. Trim wings with Black.
5. Paint butterfly's body with Black. Highlight with White.
6. Paint bee's body with Black and Yellow stripes. Highlight with white.
7. Paint bee's wings with White. Let dry.

Finish:

Seal with acrylic sealer. Let dry. ❏

continued from page 18

3. Shade with Burgundy.
4. Paint body with black. Add White highlights.
5. Add details with Black.

Paint the Black & Yellow Butterfly:
1. Paint wings with Yellow and Black.
2. Shade with Orange.
3. Highlight with White.
4. Paint body with black. Add White highlights.
5. Add details with Black.

Paint the Bee:
1. Paint body with Black and Yellow.
2. Paint wings with White.
3. Highlight body with White.

Paint the Daisy:
1. Paint petals with White.
2. Paint centers with Yellow and Orange.

Paint the Leaves:
1. Paint with Fresh Foliage.
2. Highlight with Lime.
3. Shade with Olive. Let dry.

Finish:
Seal with acrylic sealer. Let dry. ❑

Bug Pot Patterns (Actual Size)

Tulip Pot Pattern

See page 20 for instructions.

(Actual size)

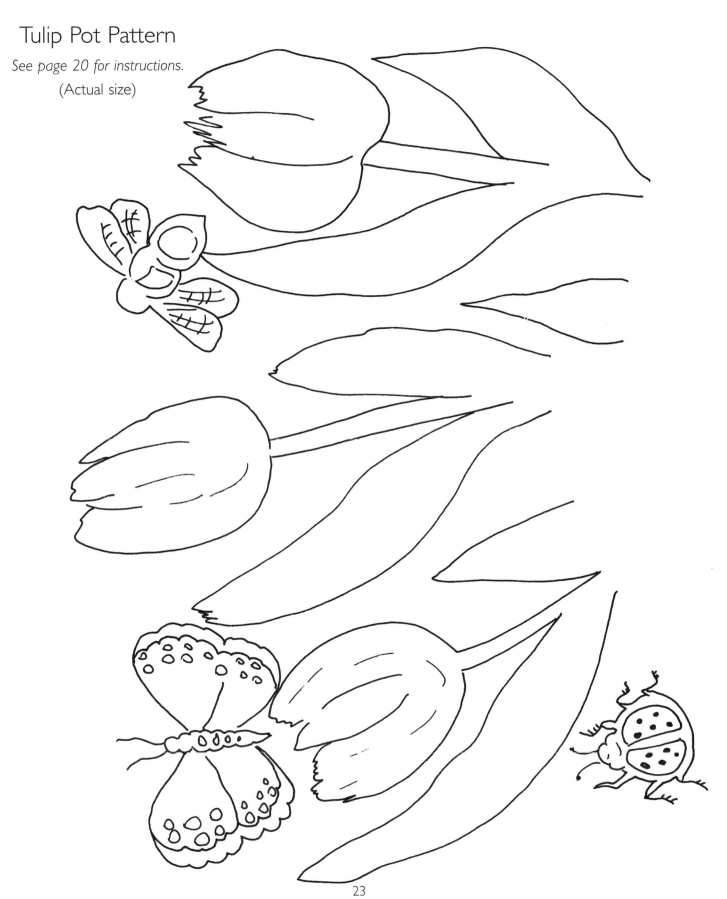

Cherry Tray Pattern

See page 21 for instructions.

Enlarge @ 135% for actual size

Rooster Pot Pattern

See page 26 for instructions.

(Actual size)

ROOSTER POT

By Holly Buttimer

Pattern on page 25

SUPPLIES

Pot:

Standard clay pot, 8"

Paints & Finishes:

Acrylic craft paints

(see color chart)

Tools & Other Supplies:

Tracing paper and pencil

Transfer paper and stylus

Glazing medium

Paint combing tool *or* graining tool

Artist brushes

INSTRUCTIONS

Base Paint:

1. Base paint pot with Lemonade.
2. Paint rim with Lime. Let dry.
3. Mix Olive paint 50/50 with glazing medium. Brush Olive paint mix over rim. While paint is still wet, comb off some of the paint with a paint comb or graining tool to create a textured look. Let dry.
4. Trace and transfer the design, repeating the motifs around the pot.

Paint the Design:

1. Basecoat roosters' feathers with Black.
2. Accent feathers with strokes of Burgundy, Sea Green, True Blue, and Olive. Highlight with Gold and White.

COLOR CHART

Lemonade	Lime	Fresh Foliage	Sea Green
Olive	Poppy Red	Tangerine	Black
Yellow	Red	Orange	Burgundy
Light Blue	True Blue	White	

3. Paint combs, wattles, and faces with Red. Highlight with Poppy Red, Orange, and White. Shade with Burgundy.
4. Paint beaks with Yellow. Highlight with Lemonade. Shade with Orange.
5. Paint eyes with Yellow. Paint pupils with black. Highlight with White.
6. Paint butterfly's wings with Orange. Highlight with Yellow and Tangerine. Shade with Burgundy.
7. Paint butterfly's body with Black. Highlight with White. Trim wings with Black.
8. Paint bee's body with Black and Yellow stripes. Highlight with White.
9. Paint bee's wings with White. Shade with Light Blue.
10. Paint flower petals with White. Paint centers with Yellow and Orange.
11. Paint leaves with Fresh Foliage. Highlight with Lime, Shade with Olive. Let dry.

Finish:

Seal with acrylic sealer. Let dry. ❑

DECOUPAGED TABLETOP FOUNTAIN

By Marie Browning

This pot was painted and decoupaged with clear transfers of old script and botanicals. A spout unit (a saucer-like base and a water spout), placed on top of the decorated pot and filled with stones, turns this pot into a fountain. The pump is hidden in the pot. The pot is covered, inside and out, with a two-part resin coating that makes it watertight.

When set, the resin coating is completely waterproof. It will, however, turn white over time if left in direct sunlight – so it's best to place it in the shade.

SUPPLIES

Pot:

Clay pot with rounded rim, 6"

Fountain Supplies:

Spout unit (saucer base and spout)

Fountain pump

Stones to fill the spout unit

Plastic tubing – enough to reach from the bottom of the pot to the spout

Paints & Finishes:

Acrylic craft paint - Buttercrunch

Two-part pour-on resin coating

Brushes:

Glue brushes, 2

1" sponge brush, need 2

Tools & Other Supplies:

Old letter or wrapping paper with script writing

Botanical prints images

4 flower-motif postage stamps

Transfer film

White glue (thin-bodied)

Wax paper

2 plastic mixing cups

2 wooden stir sticks

Large wax-coated paper cups

Bowl

Sandpaper

Continued on page 33

Assembling the Fountain

1. Insert one end of plastic tubing into spout.

2. Place other end of plastic tubing onto out-flow valve of pump.

3. Place fountain pump into pot and secure spout unit on top of pot.

DECOUPAGED FLOWER POTS

By Marie Browning

These pots are decoupaged with clear transfers of old script and botanicals on a painted surface. The pots are then covered with a two-part resin coating, making them watertight and practical for use in the garden. If you are going to plant directly in the pots, you will need to coat both inside and out with the resin.

When set, the resin coating is completely waterproof. It does, however, turn white over the years if left in direct sunlight. It is best to enjoy your finished pieces outside in a shaded area and bring them indoors during cold winters so they provide you with many years of enjoyment. Use these pots as vases, float candles in them, or use as decorative covers for plants in plastic pots.

Instructions follow on page 32.

Decoupaged Flower Pots

Pictured on page 30

SUPPLIES

Pots:

3 clay pots with rounded rims

Paints & Finishes:

Acrylic craft paints

    Buttercrunch

    Khaki Tan

Two-part pour-on resin coating

Brushes:

Glue brushes, 2

1" sponge brush

Tools & Other Supplies:

Old letter or wrapping paper with script writing

Botanical prints images (two images per pot)

Flower-motif postage stamps (four per pot)

Transfer film

White glue (thin bodied)

Wax paper

2 plastic mixing cups

2 wooden stir sticks

Large wax-coated paper cups

Paper towels

Scissors

Bowl

Sandpaper

INSTRUCTIONS

Paint & Decoupage:

1. Base paint the pots with two coats of Buttercrunch or Khaki Tan.
2. Color photocopy the script lettering and botanical images on transfer film, following the film manufacturer's instructions.
3. Tear the script transfers into 4" x 4" pieces. Place the pieces in a bowl of warm water for about 30 seconds. Remove the transfers from the water and place on the pots, sliding out the backing paper. Sponge gently with a paper towel to remove the excess moisture and smooth away any air bubbles.
4. Cut the botanical prints from the transfer paper and apply them to the pots, following the application instructions in step 3. Let the transfers dry completely.
5. Cut out the floral postal stamps and adhere to the pots.
6. With the sponge brush and the white glue, brush a coat of glue over the entire pot to seal. Two thin coats are better than one thick coat. Let dry until completely clear.

Apply the Resin Coating:

1. Cover your work surface with wax paper. Place the pots upside down on large paper cups to lift them off the work surface and allow excess resin to drip off.
2. Mix 4 oz. of pour-on resin according to the manufacturer's instructions and thickly brush on the outsides of the pots, using the glue brush and making sure the entire surface is covered.
3. Remove any bubbles by gently exhaling on the pot surface. Let the pot sit undisturbed for 24 hours to set up. Dispose of the mixing cup, stir stick, and glue brush (they can only be used once).
4. When the resin has completely set up, remove the pot from the paper cups and sand any drips away.
5. Finish the top rim and the inside of the pot with another coat of two-part resin. ❑

Decoupaged Tabletop Fountain

Pictured on page 29

INSTRUCTIONS

Decorate the Pot:

1. Base paint the pot with two coats of Buttercrunch. Let dry.
2. Color photocopy the script lettering and botanical images on transfer film, following the film manufacturer's instructions.
3. Tear the script lettering transfer into 4" x 4" pieces. Place the pieces in a bowl of warm water for about 30 seconds. Remove the transfers from the water and place on the pot, sliding out the backing paper. Sponge gently with a paper towel to remove the excess moisture and smooth away any air bubbles.
4. Cut the botanical prints from the transfer paper and apply the prints to the pot, following the application instructions in step 3. Let the transfers dry completely.
5. Cut out the floral postal stamps and adhere to the pot.
6. Using the sponge brush and white glue, brush glue over the entire pot to seal. Two thin coats are better than one thick coat. Let dry until completely clear.

Apply the Resin Coating:

1. Cover your work surface with wax paper. Place the pot on large paper cups to lift it off the work surface and allow excess resin to drip off.
2. Mix 4 oz. of pour-on resin according to the manufacturer's instructions and thickly brush on the insides of the pot, using the glue brush and making sure the entire surface is covered.
3. Turn pot upside down onto paper cups and thickly brush the outside of pot with the resin.
4. Remove any bubbles by gently exhaling on the pot surface. Let the pot sit undisturbed for 24 hours to set up. Dispose of the mixing cup, stir stick, and glue brush (they can only be used once).
5. When the resin has set up completely, remove the pot from the paper cups and sand any drips away.
6. Finish the top rim and the inside of the pot with another coat of two-part resin. Allow the resin to seal the hole in the bottom of the pot. Let dry completely.

Assemble the Fountain:

1. Insert the one end of the plastic tubing up into the spout of the spout unit.
2. Connect one end of the plastic tubing to the out-flow valve of pump.
3. Fill the pot with water.
4. Place the pump into the bottom of pot with the cord coming out the top of the pot. Fit the spout unit on top of pot.
5. Place stones in spout unit.
6. Turn pump on to activate fountain. ❏

HANGING MESSAGE POTS

By Marie Browning

These simple garden ornaments are made with small clay pots and polymer clay.
Garden words, favorite sayings, or quotes are pressed into the clay with rubber stamps.
The pots are baked, then painted and decorated.
The polymer clay sheets for the pot rims can be made with a rolling pin or a pasta machine.
Please be aware that the rolling pin or pasta machine cannot be used for food preparation
after it has been used with polymer clay.

SUPPLIES

Pots:

Small clay pots - four large size, three medium and three small

Paints & Finishes:

Acrylic craft paint - Burnt Umber

Acrylic varnish or sealer

Tools & Other Supplies:

Polymer clay - copper and gold metallic

Rubber stamp alphabet

Craft knife

Ruler

Pasta machine *or* rolling pin

White glue

Light green and dark green raffia

Preserved reindeer moss

Silk roses

Glue gun and glue sticks

Paint brushes for paint and glue

INSTRUCTIONS

Add Clay Bands to the Rims:

Gold metallic polymer clay was used on the large pot set, copper metallic on the small pot set, and an equal mix of copper and gold on the medium sized pot set.

1. Condition the polymer clay until it is soft and pliable. Run the clay through the pasta machine on the thickest setting to produce large, smooth flat sheets of polymer clay. *Option:* Roll out the clay with a wooden rolling pin to a 1/8" thickness.
2. Cut a strip of clay from the rolled sheet that is about 1/4" wider than the rim of the pot and as long as the circumference of the rim.
3. Brush a thin coat of white glue on the clay strip. Place the strip around the rim of the pot, pressing it on gently. Let the pot sit for about an hour as the white glue dries.
4. Repeat the process to cover all the pot rims with clay strips.
5. Carefully smooth out all the cut edges with your finger so the top of the pot has a smooth finish.
6. Use the rubber stamp alphabet to press letters into the clay. Use one word per pot and repeat the word all around the pot rim.

Medium pot: GARDEN FLOWERS BLOOM
Small pot: RAIN SUNSHINE RAINBOW
Large pot: SOW KINDNESS GATHER LOVE

7. Bake the pots with the polymer clay rims in the oven according to the clay manufacturer's directions. Let cool completely.

Paint & Varnish:

1. Paint the letters with a light wash of Burnt Umber, brushing the paint into the letters and gently removing the excess with a paper towel. Repeat until you are satisfied with the darkness of the letters.
2. Coat the polymer clay rims and bottoms of the pots with varnish. Let dry.

Assemble:

1. Stack the sets of pots in order, using the photo as a guide.
2. Run several strands of raffia through the drainage holes in the bottoms of the pots and tie a knot at the rim to join the pots together. Form a loop for hanging and tie to hold.
3. Decorate at the knot by adhering some preserved moss and a silk rose. ❑

WILDFLOWER BOUQUET POT SET

By Gigi Smith-Burns

Patterns on page 39

SUPPLIES

Surfaces:

4" clay rose pot

3" clay rose pot

3" standard clay pot

12" clay saucer, rectangular shaped

Paints, Mediums & Finishes:

Acrylic craft paints

    Barn Wood
    Bluebell
    English Mustard
    Italian Sage
    Lemonade
    Orchid
    Purple
    Thicket
    Thunder Blue
    Warm White
    Wicker White

Extender

Blending gel medium

Waterbase varnish

Artist Brushes:

Flats - #4, #6, #8, #10, #12 and 1" for
    applying finish

Angles - 1/2", 3/8"

Round - #3, #5

Script liner - 6/0

Tools & Other Supplies:

Tracing paper and pencil

Transfer paper and stylus

Sea sponge

INSTRUCTIONS

Base Paint & Sponge:

1. Base paint the pots with Warm White.
2. Using a sea sponge, randomly sponge with Italian Sage on the rims of the pots and inside the tray. Let dry.
3. Transfer the design lightly.

Continued on page 38

Continued from page 36

Technique Information:

I use a 1/2" angle brush for most shading and highlighting. I have extender in my brush if the paint appears to be dragging. You do not want a lot of extender in your brush, however. Blot your brush after dipping it in extender. My brush is sideloaded unless otherwise noted.

Paint the Ribbon:

The ribbon is the background color.

1. Shade inside the loops, next to the knot, on the top and bottom of the knot, and on the streamers where they come out from under something and twist and turn with Barn Wood.
2. Highlight the edges and centers of the loops, the knots, and the centers of the streamers with Wicker White.
3. Reinforce the previous shading with Barn Wood.

Paint the Leaves:

1. Basecoat the leaves with Italian Sage.

2. Shade the base of the leaf and down the center vein with Thicket.
3. Highlight opposite the shaded side of the vein with Lemonade.
4. Stroke in filler leaves with Thicket.

GIGI'S PAINTING TERMS

Sideload: Dress a flat or angle brush with extender. Dab on paper towel. Load one side of brush with the paint color. Do not allow paint to travel more than one-fourth of the way across the brush. Blend brush on wet palette.

Highlight: Highlighting lightens or brightens an area and makes that area appear closer. Use a sideloaded brush.

Shade: Shading darkens or deepens an area and usually is placed where an object turns or goes under something. I sometimes use several layers of shading, allowing each layer to stop short of the previous layer. When applying layers of shading, do not obliterate the previous shading color. The objective is to lead the eye to the deepest area.

Pivot Technique: Dress a flat or angle brush with extender and load one side with paint. Do not allow paint to travel more than one-fourth of the way across the brush. Blend brush on wet palette. With the color side of brush toward the center, gently and quickly walk the color in a circle or half circle, keeping the extender side of brush toward outer edges.

Shimmer: Place a sideloaded flat brush that has been softened on the palette on the surface and float color where the shimmer will be. Quickly reverse the process by flipping the brush and floating color against the color that was just placed. This makes the color on the outside (of both sides) fade out, leaving the center of the shimmer the brightest.

Paint the Purple Flowers:

1. Basecoat the petals with Orchid.
2. Shade the base of the petals with Purple + a touch of Orchid.
3. Highlight the tips of the petals with Warm White.
4. Paint the centers with Lemonade dots and shade with English Mustard.

Paint the Blue Flowers:

1. Basecoat the petals with Bluebell.
2. Shade the base of the petals with Thunder Blue.
3. Highlight the petals with Wicker White.

Finishing Touches:

1. Spatter all the pieces with Bluebell.
2. Apply two or more coats of waterbase varnish. ❏

Wildflower Bouquet Pot Set Pattern

(Actual size)

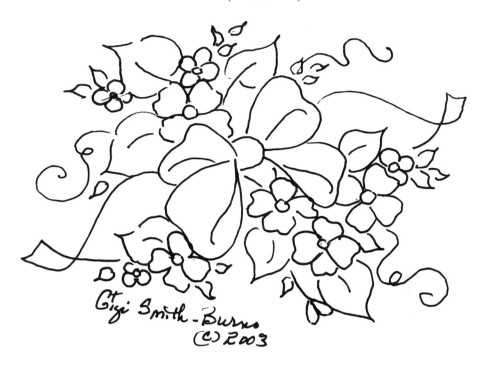

BEST FRIENDS BASKET

By Gigi Smith-Burns

A wooden handle was added to a pot to make it into a basket. The handle was cut from 1/2" pine and attached to the pot with a screw on each side. A pattern is provided for the handle.

SUPPLIES

Pot:
Standard clay pot, 8"

Paints, Mediums & Finishes:
Acrylic craft paints

Bayberry	Licorice
Burnt Sienna	Linen
Burnt Umber	Raspberry Sherbet
Buttercrunch	Rose Chiffon
Champagne	Settlers Blue
Christmas Red	Thicket
English Mustard	Warm White
Ivory White	Wicker White
Lemonade	Wrought Iron

Extender

Blending gel medium

Waterbase varnish

Artist Brushes:
Flats - #4, #6, #8, #10, #12 and 1" for applying finish

Angle - 1/2", 3/8"

Rounds - #3, #5

Filbert - #6

Rake - 1/2"

Script liner - 6/0

Tools & Other Supplies:
Wooden handle cut from 1/2" pine using jigsaw or scroll saw, pattern on page 42

2 screws, long enough to go through pot to handle

Sea sponge   Wet palette

Sandpaper   Tack cloth

Tracing paper and pencil

Transfer paper and stylus

INSTRUCTIONS

Prepare Pot and Handle:
1. Using pattern, cut out handle from wood using saw.
2. Sand edges of handle smooth. Wipe with a tack cloth.
3. Position handle on side of pot and mark inside of pot for drill holes on side of pot. Using a masonry carbide drill bit, drill holes into side of pot for insertion of screws that will hold handle in place.

Base Paint & Sponge:
1. Basecoat the pot and handle with Linen.
2. Using the sea sponge, randomly sponge both with Champagne (see photo). Let dry.
3. Transfer the design.

Paint the Hat Design:
The bunny twins are sitting in a straw hat.
1. Basecoat the hat with Buttercrunch.
2. Shade with Burnt Sienna.
3. Reinforce the previous shading with Burnt Umber. Add line work with Burnt Sienna.
4. Reinforce the shading around the rim of the hat with Wrought Iron.

Paint the Daisies:
1. Basecoat the petals with Warm White.
2. Shade the bases of petals with soft gray (Warm White + Licorice).
3. Highlight the tips of the petals with Wicker White.
4. Add lines and loosely outline the petals with Licorice.
5. Basecoat the centers with Lemonade. Shade with English Mustard + a tiny touch of Raspberry Wine.

Sponging background

6. Paint the pollen specs with Licorice.

Paint the Leaves:
1. Basecoat the leaves with Bayberry.
2. Shade the base of each leaf and down the center vein with Thicket. Highlight opposite side of vein with Lemonade (pivot technique).
3. Reinforce previous shading with Wrought Iron. Add tints of Rose Chiffon.
4. Add veins and loosely outline with Wrought Iron.

Paint the Strawberries:
1. Basecoat berries with Lemonade. Shade most of the edges with Rose Chiffon. Add some tints of Bayberry.
2. Reinforce the previous shading with Christmas Red.
3. Add seeds with Lemonade + a touch of Warm White. Add a shadow behind the seeds with Raspberry Wine. Reinforce the shading with Raspberry Wine.

continued on page 42

continued from page 40

4. Stroke the bracts using a #3 round brush loaded with Bayberry tipped into Wrought Iron.

Paint the Bunnies:
1. Shade the bunnies with a mix of Wicker White and Licorice. Color should be medium gray. Keep the shading on the ears a little darker.
2. Add fur by streaking with Ivory White, then Wicker White.
3. Paint eyes with Rose Chiffon + Raspberry Sherbet. Shade with Licorice.
4. Paint the noses with Rose Chiffon. Shade with Licorice.
5. Paint the insides of the ears with Rose Chiffon + a tiny touch of Raspberry Sherbet.
6. Paint the mouths and whiskers with Burnt Umber.

Paint the Ribbon:
The ribbon is the background color.
1. Shade the ribbon and bow with Barn Wood, shading inside the bow loops, next to the knot on the streamers, and along the twists and turns of the ribbon.
2. Highlight the edges with Warm White. Add shimmers of highlights with Wicker White.
3. Reinforce the previous shading with Barn Wood.

Finish:
1. Shade behind the design with Settlers Blue. Let dry.
2. Spatter with Raspberry Wine. Let dry.
3. Apply two or more coats of waterbase varnish.
4. Attach handle to pot with screws, screwing from inside of pot through to the handle. . ❑

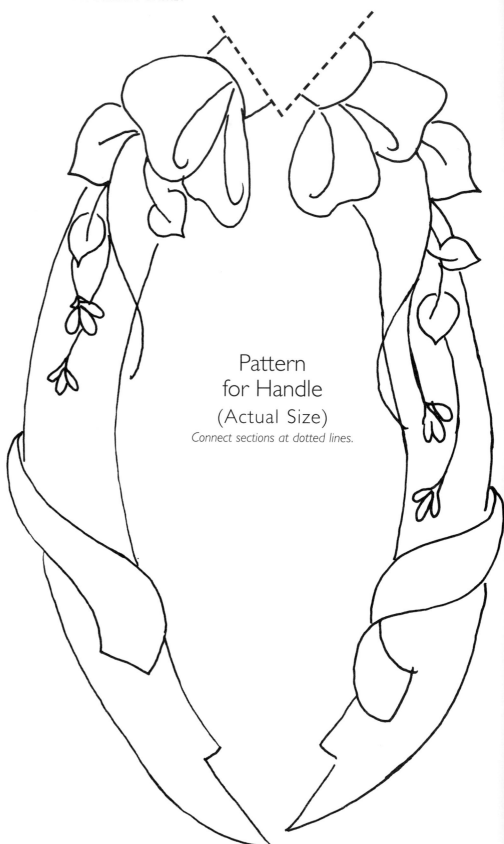

Pattern
for Handle
(Actual Size)
Connect sections at dotted lines.

Pattern for Pot
(Actual Size)

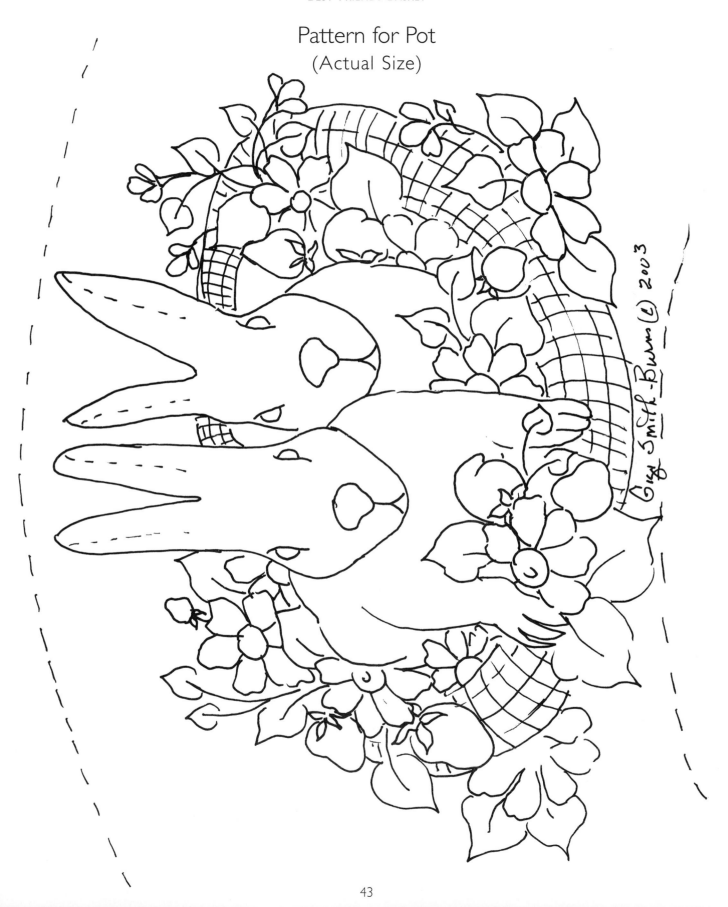

POEM POT

By Marci Donley

I used a steel-nib pen to write the words from a favorite poem around this pot – but you could use a rounded-tip permanent marker or a brush for the lettering if you prefer. For your pot, choose a favorite poem or saying. I have provided an alphabet pattern for you to use. You can reduce the letters to make a lower case one. You can highlight certain words or create an overall pattern – just play with it and have fun.

SUPPLIES

Pot:

6" standard clay pot

Paints & Finishes:

White acrylic paint

Acrylic craft paints

> Chamois
> Cherry Red
> Fresh Foliage
> Patina
> Sunflower Yellow
> Tiger Lily Orange

Writing quality black acrylic paint
(unless you opt to use a marker)

Glossy aerosol finish

Brushes:

1" foam brush

Small paint brush

Tools & Other Supplies:

Round-tip steel writing nibs - small,
medium and pen base *or* rounded-
tip permanent markers

Paper

Measuring tape

Pencil

Optional: Graphite transfer paper

INSTRUCTIONS

Prepare & Base Paint:

1. Base paint the pot with white acrylic paint, using a 1" foam brush. Paint inside the pot so it will be sealed. Let dry.
2. Paint the entire pot using the 1" brush and three shades of yellow. It works well to paint the whole pot in the middle shade and then to highlight the top and bottom with the darker shade and the middle of the pot in the lightest shade. This gives a look of texture and depth to the whole pot and a good writing surface in the middle.

Add the Lettering:

1. Measure the size of the middle area you want to write on and make a paper template. Practice your lettering on the template so you can work out your design in the space. Use the pen or brush with the paint you will be using on your pot so the spacing will match. I used two sizes of round-tip steel nibs (small and medium) and writing quality acrylic paint.
2. Hold your practice paper template on the pot above where you want to write and use it as a guide for lettering *or* transfer the words to the pot by placing graphite paper under the template and tracing the words with a stylus, then do the lettering. Let dry.

Decorate the Lettering:

Practice on a paper template before you put paint on the pot.

Choose three colors. I picked Cherry Red, Fresh Foliage, and Patina (turquoise). Using a small brush, fill in the Os and Ds and the larger spaces of some letters to create a fun and colorful pattern. Let dry.

Finish:

Spray the pot with at least two coats of spray gloss sealer. Don't forget to seal the inside of the pot. ❑

Alphabet Pattern

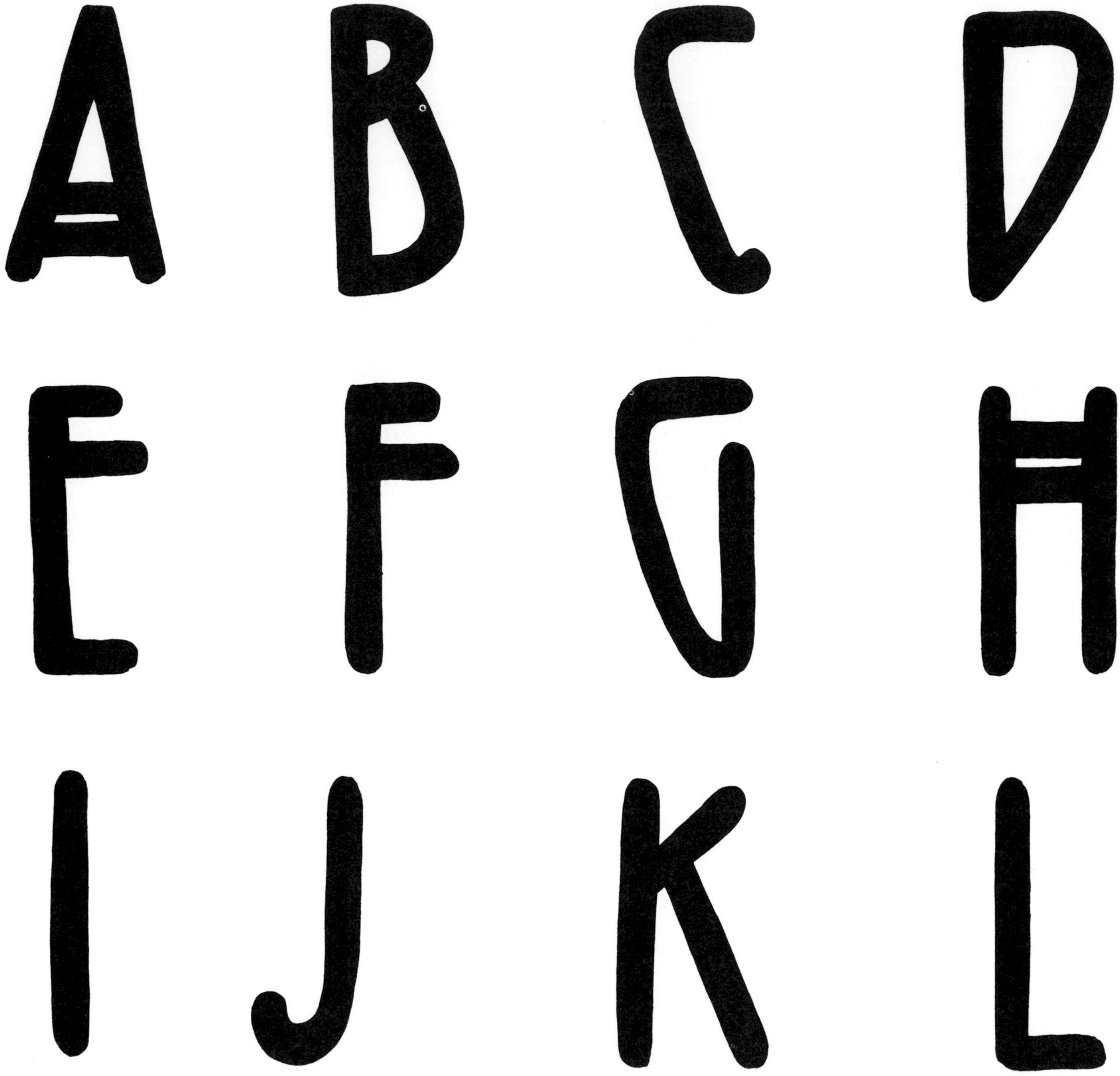

A B C D

E F G H

I J K L

Example of name insert

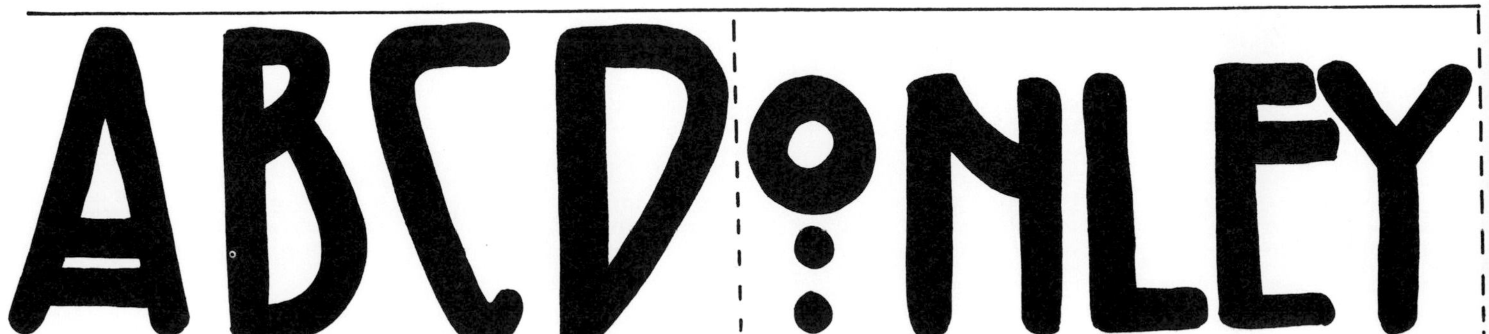

A B C D O N L E Y

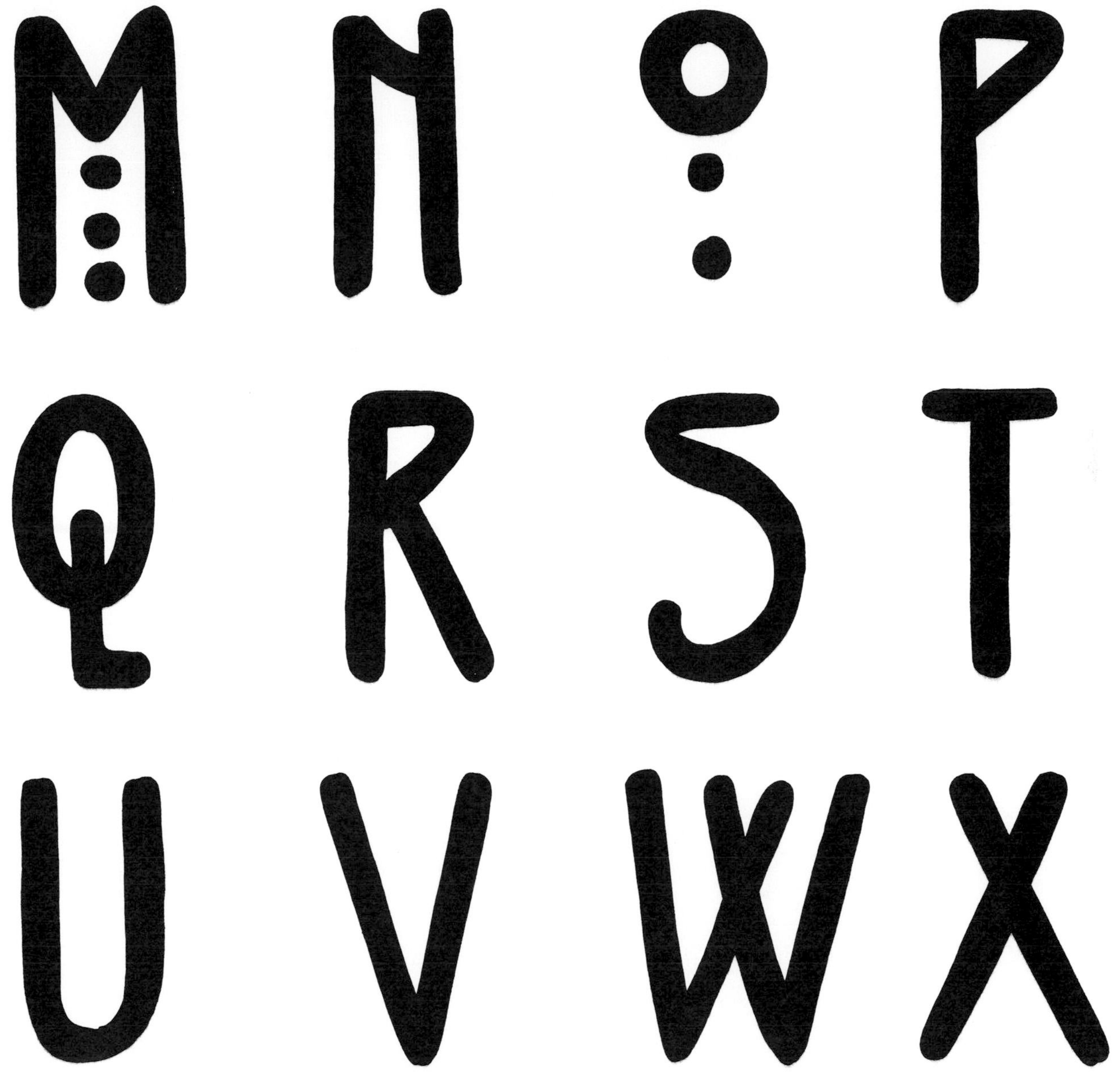

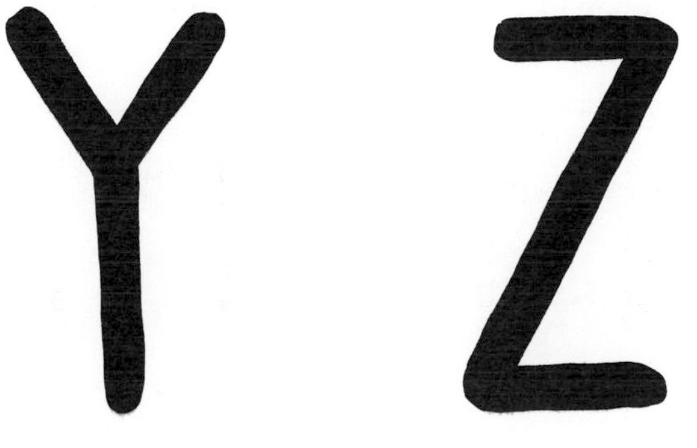

M N O P

Q R S T

U V W X

Y Z

Use this for a style of lettering for your favorite poem as shown on page 45.

Also use this same style of lettering for the Alphabet Pot on page 49.

Reduce letters for lower case.

ALPHABET POT

By Marci Donley

You can choose a lettering style you like to create the alphabet on this pot and embellish it as you like. I chose the Mackintosh alphabet, the distinctive lettering style used by Scottish architect and artist Charles Rennie Mackintosh (1868-1928). When I printed the letters, I inserted my last name, Donley, after the letter D — ABCDonleyEFGHIJKLMNOPQRSTUVWXYZ. If you're making this pot as a gift, you could include the recipient's name where it appears in the alphabet.

See pages 46 & 47 for the alphabet.

SUPPLIES

Pot:

10" standard clay pot

Paints & Finishes:

Acrylic craft paints

    Basil

    Chamois

    Eggplant

    Fairway Green

    Fresh Foliage

    Green Forest

    Old Ivy

    Orchid

    Violet Pansy

    Warm White

Spray gloss finish

Brushes:

1" foam brush

Small detail brush

1/8" artist brush

Tools & Other Supplies:

Round-tip steel writing nib - large, and pen base

Transfer paper

Masking tape

INSTRUCTIONS

Base Paint:

1. Base paint the pot with Warm White, using a 1" foam brush. Paint inside the pot to seal. Let dry.
2. Paint the entire pot using horizontal strokes with a palette of five shades of green (Old Ivy, Basil, Fairway Green, Fresh Foliage, Green Forest). Overlap the colors and use lights over darks and darks over lights to give a mottled, textured finish. Let dry.

Add the Lettering:

1. Measure the top of the pot and make a paper template as long as the circumference of the pot and the width of the rim. Use this template to practice your lettering and work out your spacing.
2. Transfer the template design to the pot.
3. Use a large round-tip steel nib with Eggplant to write the letters around the pot. Fix any ragged edges with a small detail brush.

Shade & Embellish:

1. Shade the middle of the pot with Eggplant.
2. Dry brush some Eggplant on the body of the pot to blend the design.
3. Shadow the outsides of the letters with Basil Green.
4. Paint and shade the insides of the letters with Orchid, Chamois, and Violet Pansy. Let dry.

Finish:

Spray the entire pot with gloss finish to seal. ❏

CHINESE PEACE PLANTER

By Patty Cox

SUPPLIES

Pot:

Bell-shape clay pot, 8"

Paints, Mediums & Finishes:

Spray paint - Copper

Crackle medium

Walnut stain

Clear acrylic spray sealer

Acrylic craft paints

Black
Gray-green
Off White

Tools & Other Supplies:

Paint brushes

Cloth

Tracing paper and pencil

Transfer paper and stylus

Pattern

INSTRUCTIONS

Paint:

1. Spray paint clay pot with copper paint. Let dry.

2. Paint an Off White + water wash on pot. Let dry.

3. Paint a Gray-green + water wash on pot. Let dry.

4. Transfer Chinese characters for "peace" to one side of the pot.

5. Paint characters with Black. Let dry.

Crackle & Stain:

1. Apply crackle medium according to manufacturer's instructions. Let dry.

2. Brush walnut stain over crackled surface. Wipe away with a dry cloth. Let dry.

Finish:

Spray with clear acrylic coating. Let dry. ❏

BLUEBONNET BIRDFEEDER

By Patty Cox

This birdfeeder is made using a clay pot and a funnel. The pot and funnel are painted with bluebonnets, the state flower of Texas. On the rim of the pot is a quote from Lady Bird Johnson, "Where there are flowers, there is hope."

SUPPLIES

Pot:

Standard clay pot, 6-3/4"

Clay saucer, 7"

Paints & Finishes:

Acrylic craft paints

> Green
> Light Olive
> Ultramarine Blue
> White

Gloss acrylic enamel - Chamois

Rub-on buffing wax - Metallic gold

Tools & Other Supplies:

8" metal funnel

24" x 1/4" threaded rod

2 cap nuts, 1/4"

4 fender washers, 1/4"

3 coupler nuts, 1/4"

drill and 1/4" drill bit

Expanding polyurethane foam sealant

Clear-drying multi-purpose adhesive

Paint brush

Cotton swabs

Sea sponge

Black permanent marker

24 gauge wire

INSTRUCTIONS

Assemble:

See Fig. 1.

1. Drill a 1/4" hole in the center of saucer.
2. Glue saucer to base of clay pot.
3. Assemble threaded rod through pot and saucer. Add a fender washer to rod on each side of clay pot and saucer. Secure base of rod with a cap nut. Secure washer inside of pot with nut.
4. Add a nut and fender washer to top of rod. Screw nut down rod about 4".
5. Slide funnel over top of rod. Secure funnel tightly at top by adding a fender washer, coupler nut, and cap nut.
6. Wrap 28 gauge wire into a 1" loop. Wrap loop three times. Add hanging loop under top cap nut, wrapping ends around rod. Tighten cap nut securely over wire.
7. Spray about 1" of polyurethane foam in bottom inside of pot. (It will rise to about 3".)

Paint the Design:

See the Bluebonnet Birdfeeder Worksheet.

1. Paint entire piece with Chamois. Let dry.
2. Using the sea sponge, lightly sponge foliage around base of pot and funnel with Green and Light Olive.
3. Double load a cotton swab with Ultramarine Blue and White. Make dots to represent the flowers, forming

Continued on page 54

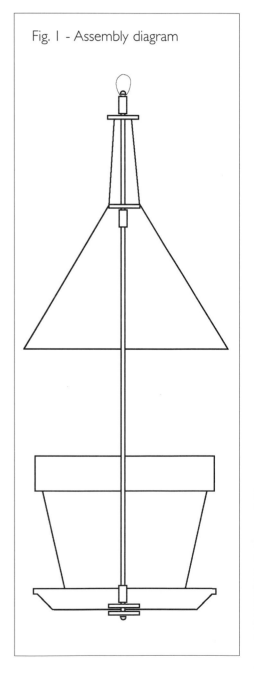

Fig. 1 - Assembly diagram

continued from page 52

the dots in a cone shape. Place the dots so that the white paint is on the top of each dot.

4. Paint leaves, using a brush, with Light Olive and Green.
5. Using the handle end of a paint brush, dot tiny Ultramarine Blue bluebonnets on sponged foliage.

Finish:

1. Transfer quotation to rim of pot. Write with a permanent black marker.
2. Rub gold metallic wax along top rim of pot and along rim and top of funnel. Let dry.
3. Spray with clear acrylic finish. ❏

Bluebonnet Worksheet

'Where there are flowers, there is hope.' Lady Bird Johnson

FAUX RAKU POT

By Patty Cox

Raku is a high-heat ceramic firing process that originated in Japan that involves the use of metallic glazes and ashes. The painted finish of this pot mimics the raku look with metallic paint and masking fluid.

SUPPLIES

Pot:

Clay pot, 8-1/2"

Paints & Finishes:

Gold spray paint

Clear acrylic spray sealer

Acrylic craft paint - Russet

Metallic acrylic paints

　Ice Blue
　Plum Pearl
　Purple Pearl
　Turquoise Pearl

Tools & Other Supplies:

Sea Sponge

Colorless art masking fluid

Paint brushes

INSTRUCTIONS

1. Spray paint clay pot with Gold. Let dry.
2. Drip art masking fluid on selected areas around pot, using the photo as a guide. Let dry.
3. Sponge pot with metallic paints mixed with Russet. Let dry.
4. Rub masking fluid away with your fingers.
5. Spray with acrylic coating. Let dry. ❏

BLUE FEATHERS PLANTER

By Patty Cox

Patterns on page 58

SUPPLIES

Pot:

Clay azalea pot, 8-1/2"

Paints, Mediums & Finishes:

Acrylic craft paints

   Gold (metallic)
   Light Turquoise
   Turquoise
   Ultramarine Blue
   White

Blending gel medium

Clear acrylic spray sealer

Tools & Other Supplies:

16 turquoise glass half marbles

Clear-drying multi-purpose glue

Paint brushes

Heavy paper

Scissors

Tracing paper

INSTRUCTIONS

Base Paint & Transfer Designs:

1. Paint clay pot with Light Turquoise. Let dry.
2. Divide perimeter of pot into 16 sections.
3. Trace teardrop-shaped feather pattern. Cut out pattern from heavy paper to make a template.
4. Place template on side of pot. Trace around template to make 16 feathers side by side.
5. Trace scallop pattern and cut out from heavy paper to make a template. Position template on rim and trace around template to make 16 scallops on the rim.

Paint the Design:

1. Paint teardrop shapes and scallops with Turquoise. Let dry.
2. Paint feather design and outline feathers with Ultramarine Blue. Float Ultramarine Blue to the right of each feather, to the right side of each feather center quill, and along the inner edge of each scallop.
3. Mix Turquoise + White. Paint feather center quill. With the light turquoise mix, add highlights on top left and lower right side of each feather.
4. Mix Gold + blending medium. Add highlights at top left of each feather. Let dry.

Finish:

1. Glue half marbles around top edge of pot inside each scallop. Let dry.
2. Spray with clear acrylic finish. ❏

Blue Feathers Planter Pattern
(Actual Size)

See page 56 for instructions.

Scallop template

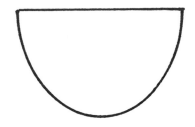

Feather
template

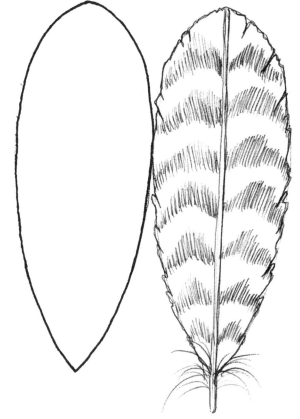

Feather
painting pattern

Laughter Pot Pattern
(Actual Size)
See page 60 for instructions.

LAUGHTER POT

By Marci Donley

Pattern on page 59

SUPPLIES

Pot:

Standard clay pot, 8"

Paints & Finishes:

Acrylic craft paints

    Black

    Cadmium Yellow

    Calico Red

    Eggplant

    Fresh Foliage

    Orchid

    Pediment Gray

    Tiger Lily Orange

    Warm White

    White

Glossy spray finish

Brushes:

Flats - 1", 1/2", 1/8"

Script

Round - 00

Tools & Other Supplies:

Round sponge-on-a-stick applicator, 3/4"

Black permanent marker

Buttons, charms, flat-backed glass marbles (for embellishments)

Multi-purpose glue

Measuring tape

Ruler

Pencil

Sheet of paper

Graphite transfer paper

INSTRUCTIONS

Base Paint & Measure:

1. Base paint the pot with Warm White, using a 1" paint brush. Paint inside the pot to seal. Let dry.
2. Paint the whole pot with Calico Red.
3. Measure the circumference of the rim of the pot to determine the size of the squares for the checkerboard pattern. My pot measured 26-3/4" and the rim was 1-1/2" wide so I made the checks 3/4" squares. Once you determine the size of the squares, use a ruler and pencil to draw the lines on the rim. If the measurements of your pot don't divide equally, adjust the size of the squares so the checkerboard looks visually correct.

Paint the Design:

1. Paint every other square on the top row with Black, using the 1/2" flat brush. Then paint the bottom row to form the checkerboard pattern.
2. Highlight the right side of every black square with White, using the script brush. (This helps the squares "pop" off the surface.) Let dry.
3. Paint circles around the bottom of the pot using the sponge-on-a-stick applicator with Black paint. Let dry.
4. Wrap a piece of paper around the middle of the pot to determine the size and shape of the area on which you will place the lettering. Make a paper template of this size and shape.
5. Use the template to work out the style and size of the words. (You can use the pattern provided or write words that inspire you.) Position the template on the pot with graphite paper underneath it and transfer the word designs to the pot.
6. Paint the letters.
   - "Laugh" - Use the 1/8" brush with Cadmium Yellow to write the word. Go over the letters with Tiger Lily Orange to make a thicker letter and add depth. Shadow the left sides of the letters with Pediment Gray. Highlight the right sides with Warm White. Add Eggplant dots. Add details with a black marker.
   - "Live" - Outline the letters with a black marker. Use the 1/8" brush to fill in with Cadmium Yellow and Tiger Lily Orange. Shadow the left sides of the letters with Pediment Gray. Highlight the right sides with Warm White. Add Eggplant dots, using the handle end of the brush or the OO brush.
   - "Create" - Write the word with Eggplant, using the script brush. Add layers of Orchid and Fresh Foliage to make the letters thicker. Outline the letters with a black marker. Highlight with Warm White. Finish off the letters with dots of Eggplant and Tiger Lily Orange.

Finish:

1. Embellish the pot by gluing on buttons, charms, and glass flat-back marbles.
2. Spray with a few coats of glossy finish to seal both the inside and the outside of the pot. Let dry. ❑

To decorate this pot, I wrote the words LAUGH, LIVE, and CREATE in three different styles and placed them around the pot, then added a small circle between each word. You could place it anywhere in your house that you need some inspiration.

FROSTED GAZING BALL

By Patty Cox

SUPPLIES

Pots & Saucers:

Rose clay pot, 4"

Azalea clay pot, 4-1/4"

Clay saucer, 6-3/4"

Clay saucer, 3"

Paints, Mediums & Finishes:

Crackle medium

Spray paint - White Frost

Clear acrylic spray sealer

Acrylic craft paints

    Evergreen

    Mint Green

Tools & Other Supplies:

Wood finial, 4-1/2" tall

Round glass votive, 5-1/2" diameter

Expanding polyurethane foam sealant

Clear-drying multi-purpose glue

Paint brushes

Serrated knife

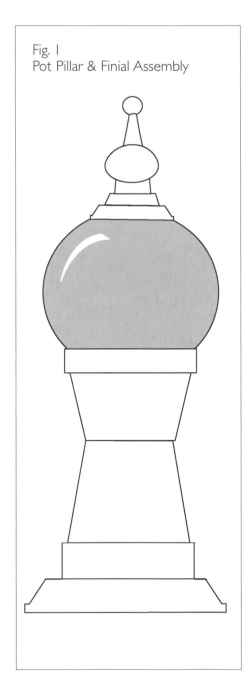

Fig. I
Pot Pillar & Finial Assembly

INSTRUCTIONS

See the Assembly Diagram, Fig. 1.

Assemble the Pot Pillar & Finial:

1. Glue rose pot base to the azalea pot base. Let dry.
2. Spray polyurethane foam in pots for added strength. Let dry.
3. Trim expanded foam evenly with each pot rim, using a serrated knife.
4. Glue 6-3/4" saucer at pillar base.
5. Glue wood finial to bottom of 3" clay saucer.

Paint:

1. Spray glass votive with White Frost spray paint. Set aside to dry.
2. Paint pot pillar and finial with Evergreen. Let dry.
3. Following manufacturer's instructions, brush crackle medium over paint. Let dry.
4. Topcoat with Mint. Cracks will form. Let dry.
5. Spray painted pillar and finial with clear acrylic coating. Let dry.

Assemble:

1. Glue glass votive to pillar top, with open side of votive facing down.
2. Glue finial with 3" saucer to votive top. Let dry. ❑

COVERED BUTTERFLY CONTAINER

By Karen Embry

An upside-down saucer makes a perfect cover for a clay pot – simply add a knob or finial.
A covered pot is a wonderful container for a patio candle, and it's a perfect package for
a gift – fill it with bath products like fragrant soaps and bath salts or with homemade
cookies, savory snacks, or candies in cellophane bags.

Patterns on page 66

SUPPLIES

Pot:

Standard clay pot, 8-1/2"

Clay saucer (The top of the saucer
should fit the top of the pot.)

Paints, Mediums & Finishes:

Acrylic craft paints
　Basil Green
　Berries 'n Cream
　Gray Plum
　Inca Gold (metallic)

Sparkle paint - Gold Glitter

Glazing medium

Antiquing medium - Apple Butter
　Brown

Brush-on satin sealer

Brushes:

#8 mop

Wash, 1"

Tools & Other Supplies:

Wooden knob, 1-1/2"

Butterfly motif stencil *or* stencil blank
　material, craft knife, and fine tip
　marker

Small plastic bottle

Small palette knife

White craft glue

Modeling paste

INSTRUCTIONS

Prepare & Base Paint:

1. Wipe dust from clay pot and saucer.
2. Apply two coats of brush-on satin sealer to pot and saucer. Let dry.

Stencil:

Use a purchased stencil or cut one of your own using the pattern provided.

1. Position stencil on pot. Using a palette knife, apply a thin layer of molding paste to butterfly areas of stencil, leaving a raised pattern of the stencil design. Lift stencil.
2. Move the stencil around the pot and create more butterflies with the molding paste all around the pot. Let dry completely.

Paint:

1. Brush glazing medium over entire pot and saucer. Apply patches of Berries 'n Cream, Gray Plum, and Basil Green paint. Blend just the edges of the colors together with a mop brush. Do not blend colors completely – you should still be able to see all three colors.
2. Paint band around saucer and wooden knob with Inca Gold.
3. Apply two coats of Gold Glitter sparkle paint to the butterflies. Let dry between coats.

Finish:

1. Glue wooden knob to saucer.
2. Apply two coats of brush-on satin sealer. Let dry. ❑

Covered Butterfly Container Pattern
(Actual Size)

See page 64 for instructions.

Wedding Shower Gift Container Pattern
(Actual Size)

See page 68 for instructions.

To have and to hold ...

WEDDING SHOWER GIFT CONTAINER

By Karen Embry

Pattern on page 67

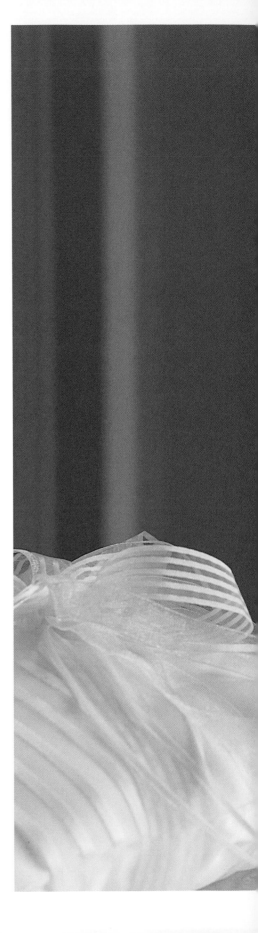

SUPPLIES

Pot:

Clay azalea pot, 8-1/2"

Paints & Finishes:

Acrylic craft paints

    Taupe (metallic)

    Wicker White

Glitter paint - Hologram

Spray satin sealer

Brushes:

Wash, 1"

#3 round

Tools & Other Supplies:

Stencil with heart and bird motifs *or* stencil blank material, craft knife, and fine tip marker

Modeling paste

Tracing paper and pencil

Transfer paper and stylus

Palette knife

Cotton cloth

INSTRUCTIONS

Prepare:

Wipe clay pot with a damp cloth to remove dust.

Stencil:

Use a purchased stencil or make your own using the patterns provided.

Position stencil on pot. Spread molding paste thinly with palette knife over heart and bird motifs. Remove stencil carefully. Let dry completely.

Paint the Design:

1. Paint pot with Wicker White.
2. Paint rim with Taupe. Let rim dry completely.
3. Trace and transfer lettering pattern.
4. Dry brush inside of pot with Taupe.
5. Dry brush the white area on outside of pot with Taupe. Before paint dries, wipe it off with a dry cotton cloth to achieve an antiqued look. Allow the paint to settle in the areas around the stenciled designs.
6. Paint the raised stenciled design (heart and birds) and lettering with Wicker White. Let dry.

Finish:

1. Spray pot with two coats of satin sealer. Let dry between coats.
2. Apply two coats of brush-on Hologram glitter paint to birds and heart. ❑

RUSTIC GARDEN FAIRY

By Patty Cox

SUPPLIES

Pot:

Clay azalea pot, 4-1/4"

Paints & Finishes:

Clear acrylic spray sealer

Spray paint - Rust

Acrylic craft paints

    Burnt Sienna

    Raw Sienna

Tools & Other Supplies:

1 metal rod, 24" x 1/4"

1 fender washer, 1/4"

4" hinge

Serving-size spoon

2 oyster forks

2 spring tube benders, 3/8"

Hanger wire

Clear-drying multi-purpose glue

Expanding polyurethane foam sealant

Metal wings

24 gauge wire

Needlenose pliers

Sea sponge

8 round star charms, 1"

Fine-tip permanent black marker

INSTRUCTIONS

Assemble:

Refer to Figures 1 - 3 on page 72.

1. Slide rod through bottom hole of clay pot, extending it about 3-3/4" (the folded length of the hinge).
2. Slide fender washer over rod on inside of clay pot.
3. Lay clay pot, with rod inside, on its side. Glue fender washer to inside of clay pot. Glue rod to washer, using a generous amount of glue. Lift long end of rod about 1" away from side of clay pot. Use a serving spoon to prop it until the glue dries. See Fig. 1.
4. Bend hanger wire into a curve for other leg. See Fig. 2. Bend the hook and hanger top into a coil. Glue coiled end inside pot. Slip spring tube benders over "legs" and glue in place. See Fig. 3. Let glue dry.
5. Spray inside of pot with polyurethane foam. Let dry.
6. Bend oyster forks (the fairy's arms) at "elbows" and at "finger" tines. Glue oyster forks inside hinge (the fairy's "shoulders").
7. Fold hinge over 1/4" rod where it protrudes from the pot. Glue in position.
8. Glue tablespoon over front center of hinge.
9. Glue metal wings on hinge back. Let dry.

Paint:

1. Spray entire garden fairy with Rust spray paint. Let dry.
2. Sponge Raw Sienna and Burnt Sienna over paint to give the appearance of rusted metal. Let dry.

Finish:

1. Spray fairy with crystal clear acrylic. Let dry.
2. Draw face on spoon with fine-tip permanent marker.
3. Glue star charms around rim of pot skirt, spacing them 1-3/4" apart.
4. To make the halo, wrap 24 gauge wire around a 2 oz. paint tube seven times. Cut ends and twist together. Slightly flatten wires into a narrow oval shape. Glue halo loops on back of spoon "head."
5. Wrap 24 gauge wire in a criss cross around the angel's torso seven times. Cut ends and twist together in back. ❏

Rustic Garden Fairy

Pictured on page 71

Assembly Diagrams

Fig. 1

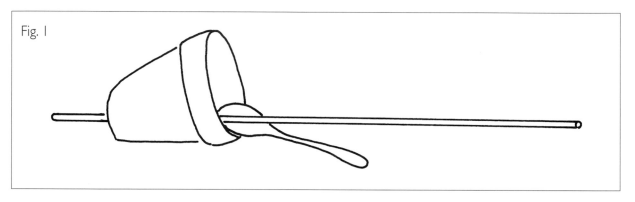

Fig. 2

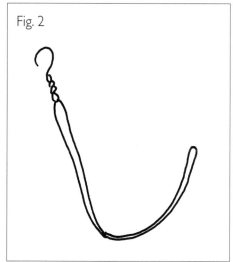

Pattern for Face (actual size)

Fig. 3

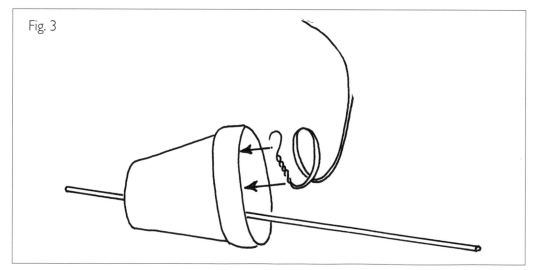

Bamboo Planter Pattern

See page 74 for instructions.

Enlarge pattern @145% for actual size.

BAMBOO PLANTER

By Patty Cox

Pattern on page 73

SUPPLIES

Pot:

Clay pot, 10"

Paints & Finishes:

Crackle medium

Acrylic wood stain - Light Oak

Clear acrylic spray sealer

Acrylic craft paints

> Christmas Green
> Deep Forest Green

Indoor/outdoor acrylic enamel - Mustard

Tools & Other Supplies:

Paint brushes

Tracing paper and pencil

Transfer paper and stylus

Paper towel

INSTRUCTIONS

Base Paint & Prepare:

1. Paint clay pot with Mustard. Let dry.
2. Trace and transfer the design.

Paint the Design:

1. Paint bamboo with Christmas Green. Use the photo as a guide – add water to paint when painting the background leaves so they will appear transparent.
2. Float Deep Forest Green to shade. Let dry.

Crackle:

Apply crackle medium according to manufacturer's instructions. Allow to dry. Cracks will form.

Stain:

Apply light oak stain to pot. Rub away excess with a paper towel. Let dry.

Finish:

Spray with clear acrylic finish. ❏

ST. FRANCIS BIRDFEEDER & BIRDBATH

By Patty Cox

Pattern on page 79

SUPPLIES

Pots & Saucers:

Rose clay pot, 4"

2 standard clay pots, 3"

Standard clay pot, 2"

Standard clay pot, 1-3/4"

Clay saucer, 4"

Clay saucer, 8"

Paints & Finishes:

Acrylic craft paints

    Bright Green

    Burnt Sienna

    Ebony Black

    Georgia Clay

    Grey Sky

    Mistletoe

    Moon Yellow

    Neutral Gray

    Sable Brown

    Spice Pink

    White

Clear acrylic spray sealer

Tools & Other Supplies:

Spring tube bender

Hanger wire

Expanding polyurethane foam sealant

Clear-drying multi-purpose glue

Paint brushes

Serrated-edge knife

Compressed sponge

Tracing paper and pencil

Transfer paper and stylus

You can put birdseed in the "hat" or fill it with water to make a birdbath. He is holding a pot that can be filled with birdseed.

INSTRUCTIONS

Assemble:

Refer to Figures 1 - 2 on page 78.

1. For the head and hat, glue 8" saucer on top of 3" clay pot. (Fig. 1) Glue 1-3/4" pot, rim down, on top saucer at center.
2. For the cassock and arms, glue 3" pot on base of 4" rose pot.
3. Cut hook from hanger wire. Slide wire through spring tube bender. Bend spring into a curve. Insert wire ends into hole of small clay pot. (Fig. 1) Secure inserted wire with glue.
4. Spray inside of 4" saucer with polyurethane foam. Let dry.
5. Trim expanded foam evenly with saucer rim using a serrated knife.
6. Generously apply glue over inserted wire and base of 3" pot. Center and press 4" saucer (shoulder) over pot and wire.
7. Center and glue head on shoulders. (Fig. 2) Let glue dry.
8. Trace and transfer the patterns.

Paint the Design:

1. Paint robe, hat rim, and hat top with Burnt Sienna.
2. Paint hair with Grey Sky. Shade with Ebony Black and Neutral Gray.
3. Paint skin with Georgia Clay. Shade with Burnt Sienna.
4. Paint rope with Moon Yellow. Shade with Sable Brown.
5. Paint frog with Bright Green. Shade with Mistletoe.
6. Paint bunny and all eyes with White. Shade bunny with Grey Sky.
7. Paint bunny's ears and nose with Spice Pink.
8. Using the pattern provided, cut a square from the compressed sponge. Dampen to expand. Use the sponge to stamp diamonds with Georgia Clay.
9. Shade diamonds with Burnt Sienna.

Finish:

1. Glue a 1-3/4" clay pot in arms. (It can be filled with bird seed.)
2. Spray with clear acrylic sealer. ❏

Assembly Diagrams

Fig. 1 - The pieces of the birdfeeder & birdbath

Fig. 2 - The birdfeeder & birdbath assembled

Patterns for St. Francis
Birdfeeder & Birdbath
(Actual Size)

Sponge

HYDRANGEAS & HUMMINGBIRD PLANTER

By Patty Cox

Pattern on page 82

SUPPLIES

Pot:

Standard clay pot, 10"

Paints, Mediums & Finishes:

Pre-mixed transparent paint glazes

    Bluebell
    Danish Blue
    Ivy Green
    New Leaf Green
    Pale Violet

Glazing medium

Acrylic craft paints

    Deep Blue
    Plum
    Purple

Gloss acrylic enamel - Chamois

Clear acrylic spray sealer

Tools & Other Supplies:

Pre-cut foam stamping blocks -
    Lilac/Hydrangeas motif

Paint brushes

Sponge

INSTRUCTIONS

Base Paint & Sponge:

1. Basecoat pot with Chamois. Let dry.
2. Sponge rim with Deep Blue and Plum.

Stamp:

Stamp hydrangeas and leaves around the base of the pot, using the transparent glazes. Use a flat brush to load the stamping blocks with mixes of Bluebell, Danish Blue, and Pale Violet for the flowers and Ivy Green and New Leaf Green for the leaves. Use more glaze on the flowers and leaves in the foreground and less on the ones in the background, loading the glazes just on the edges. See Example.

Paint:

1. Float Deep Blue shadows around groups of hydrangeas and under leaves, using photo as a guide. Let dry.
2. Transfer hummingbird pattern.
3. Add neutral glazing medium to acrylic paints so paints are somewhat transparent.
4. Paint body, beak, eye, and left wing of hummingbird with Deep Blue + glazing medium, letting some of the base paint show through.

Painting Example
Stamped Background Flowers

5. Paint hummingbird's head, right wing, and back with Purple + glazing medium.
6. Lightly float wing motion lines behind wings with glazing medium + a touch of Purple. Let dry.

Finish:

Spray with clear acrylic finish. ❏

Hydrangeas & Hummingbird Planter Pattern
(Actual Size)

See page 80 for instructions.

Whimsical Birdfeeder Pattern
(Actual Size)

See page 84 for instructions.

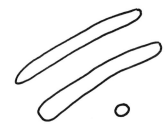

Design for decorating wings

Design for decorating pot

Whimsical Birdfeeder Patterns

(Actual Size)

Pattern for tail
Cut 1 from plastic milk jug

Pattern for wing
Cut 2 from plastic milk jug

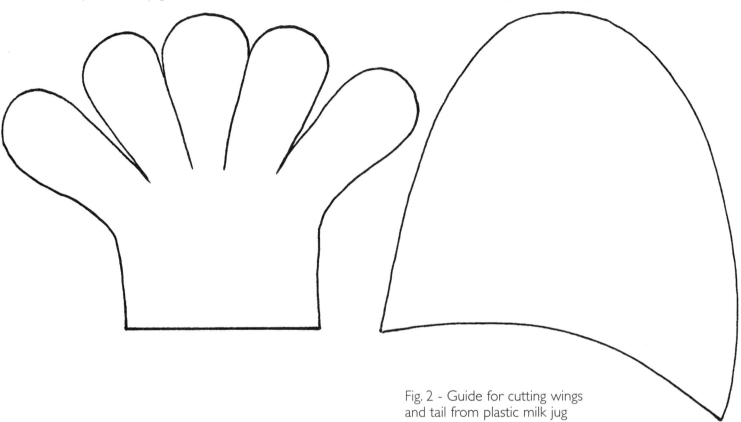

Fig. 2 - Guide for cutting wings
and tail from plastic milk jug

Fig. 1 - Guide for cutting funnel

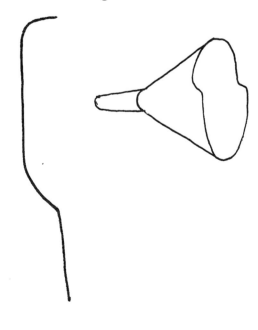

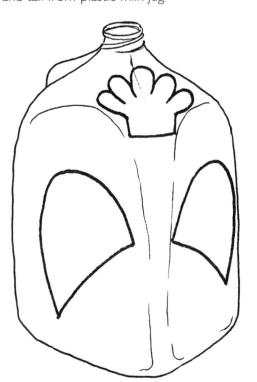

Whimsical Birdfeeder

By Patty Cox

Wings and a tail cut from a plastic milk jug and a beak cut from a plastic funnel transform a standard clay pot into a fun, colorful birdfeeder. For durability, use paint specially made for the wings and tail.

Pattern on pages 82 and 83

SUPPLIES

Pot:

Clay azalea pot, 8-1/2"

Paints & Finishes:

Gloss indoor/outdoor acrylic paints

Ink Blue

Mustard

Acrylic paint for plastic

Bright Yellow

Red

Clear acrylic spray sealer

Tools & Other Supplies:

3-1/2" yellow plastic funnel

One-gallon milk jug

1 threaded rod, 24" x 5/16"

2 fender washers, 5/16"

2 coupler nuts, 5/16"

Clear-drying multi-purpose adhesive

Expanding polyurethane foam sealant

Paint brushes

Spring tube bender, 5/8"

2 wiggle eyes, 25mm

Serrated-edge knife

Large rubber bands

Black permanent marker

Disposable foam plate

Scissors

INSTRUCTIONS

Assemble Pot & Beak:

1. Paint pot with Ink Blue. Let dry.
2. Insert rod through center bottom hole in pot. Extend end of rod about 4" inside pot.
3. Slide fender washers on each end of rod. Add coupler nuts on each end of rod. Tighten washers on each side of pot base.
4. Cut wide end of plastic funnel to conform to the top rim of pot. See Fig. 1 (page 83).
5. Fill inside of funnel, inside of tube bender, and inside of pot with expanding foam. Let dry.
6. Using a serrated knife, cut expanded foam even with the cut edges of funnel, conforming the shape to the shape of the clay pot rim.
7. Glue funnel to top side of pot, using photo as a guide. Secure in place with a large rubber bands until dry.
8. Using a black permanent marker, add the lines on the beak, using the photo as a guide.

Paint & Decorate:

1. Cut two plastic wings and one tail from plastic milk jug, using the patterns provided. See Fig. 2 (page 83).
2. Paint all sides of wings with Bright Yellow paint for plastic. Paint tail with Red paint for plastic. Let dry.
3. Paint wiggly lines and dots on wings with Red paint for plastic. Let dry.
4. Paint spirals on sides of pot with Mustard. Let dry.
5. Glue wings on sides of pot, under lip of rim.
6. Glue tail on inside back of pot.

Finish:

1. Slide spring tube bender on rod. Glue in place under clay pot.
2. Spray birdfeeder with clear acrylic finish.
3. Cut a 6-3/4" circle from a foam plate. Glue in position over polyurethane foam, making a flat surface to hold birdseed. Let dry.
4. Glue wiggle eyes in position.

To use: Insert rod in garden soil. Fill feeder with bird seed. ❑

CARPE DIEM POT

By Marci Donley

To create the design around the bottom of the pot, I consulted a book of ancient symbols and chose the old Roman symbols for the days of the week. I thought they worked well with the Latin motto *Carpe Diem et Tempus Fugit*, which means "Seize the Day and Time Flies."

Pattern on pages 88 and 89

SUPPLIES

Pot:

8" standard clay pot

Paints, Mediums & Finishes:

Crackle medium

Metallic acrylic craft paints

    Antique Copper
    Blue Pearl
    Garnet Red
    Gunmetal Gray

Acrylic craft paint - Warm White

Writing quality acrylic paint - Prussian Blue

Spray gloss finish

Brushes:

1" foam brush

1/8" flat brush

Tools & Other Supplies:

Steel nib, 5 mm, and pen base

Tracing paper

Transfer paper and stylus

Paper (for templates)

Measuring tape

INSTRUCTIONS

Base Paint & Crackle:

1. Base paint the pot with Warm White, using a 1" foam brush. Paint inside the pot to seal. Let dry.
2. Apply crackle medium to the pot over the base paint, following the manufacturer's instructions. Let dry as directed.
3. Brush with Antique Copper to create the look of an old bronze pot.

Practice & Paint:

1. Measure the top of the pot and make a paper template the width of the pot's rim and the length of its circumference. Use this template to practice the lettering. Use the pattern provided for the letter shapes and adjust the pattern as needed to fit your pot.
2. Transfer the design to the pot.
3. Write your letters on the rim of the pot, using a 5mm nib with Prussian Blue. *Option:* Use a brush. Let dry.
4. Add a shadow on the left side of each letter with Gunmetal Gray, using a 1/8" flat brush.
5. Embellish the letters with Garnet Red by dipping the end of the brush in the paint and putting dots on the letters all around the pot.
6. Accent the insides of the diamonds between the words with Blue Pearl.
7. Make another template for the bottom of the pot using the pattern provided and follow the same process to put symbols, diamonds, and dots on the bottom of the pot. Let dry.

Finish:

Seal the pot with a few coats of gloss spray finish. Let dry. ❏

Carpe Diem Pot Pattern

(Actual Size)

See page 86 for instructions.

Carpe Diem

Tempus Fugit

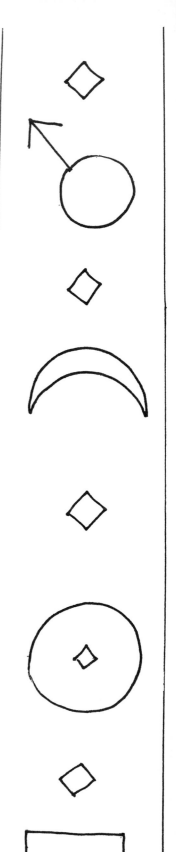

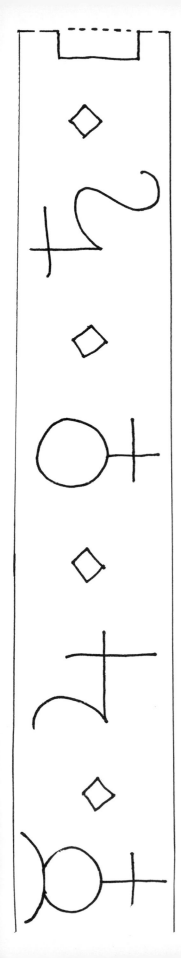

Erin Go Braugh Pot Pattern

(Actual Size)

See page 90 for instructions.

Erin Go Braugh Pot

By Marci Donley

Erin go braugh means "Forever Ireland." I chose Uncial lettering because it is the style found in many old Celtic books.

SUPPLIES

Pot:

4" clay rose pot

Paints, Mediums & Finishes:

Crackle medium

Acrylic craft paints

  Basil Green
  Cherry Red
  Fresh Foliage
  Gold (metallic)
  Green Forest
  Patina Blue
  Warm White

Bleed-proof paint - White

Spray gloss finish

Brushes:

1" brush

Small detail brush

Tools & Other Supplies:

Steel nib, 5mm, and pen base

Paper (for template)

Tracing paper

Transfer paper and stylus

Measuring tape

INSTRUCTIONS

Base Paint & Crackle:

1. Base paint with Warm White, using a 1" paint brush. Paint inside the pot to seal. Let dry.
2. Apply crackle medium over the base paint, following the manufacturer's instructions. Let dry as directed.
3. Brush on a palette of three shades of green to add depth and age to the color, using the 1" brush. Keep the mix simple so you don't overpower or obliterate the crackled look.

Add the Design:

1. Measure the top of the pot and make a paper template the width of the pot's rim and the length of the circumference. Use this template to practice your lettering, using the pattern provided. Adjust the pattern as needed to fit your pot. *Tip:* Practice with the writing tool and paint you plan to use on the pot.
2. Transfer the design to the rim of the pot.
3. Write your letters in White bleed-proof paint on the rim of the pot. *Option:* Use a 1/8" flat brush for lettering. Let dry.
4. Fill in the counter-spaces (the insides of the letters) with Cherry Red, Fresh Foliage, and Patina Blue, using the small detail brush. (I was thinking of the Book of Kells when I added this.)
5. Dip the end of the brush into Gold and put the dots between the letters. Form triangles of three gold dots between the words.
6. Use the handle end of the brush and all the colors to form a pattern with dots about 1" below the rim of the pot. Use the photo as a guide. Let dry.

Finish:

Seal with a few coats of glossy spray finish. Don't forget to seal the inside of the pot. ❏

DECORATED CANDLE HOLDER

By Karen Embry

SUPPLIES

Pots:

2 cylinder clay pots, 4-3/4"

Paints, Mediums & Finishes:

Acrylic craft paints

   Antique Gold (metallic)

   Light Gray

Brush-on satin sealer

Glass and tile medium

Brushes:

Wash, 1"

#3 round

Tools & Other Supplies:

Tracing paper

Transfer paper and stylus

White craft glue

1/2 yd. sheer white ribbon with pearls, 1" wide

Assorted clear white rhinestones

Assorted gold filigree and pearl buttons

White pillar candle, 8" tall

Patterns
(Actual Size)

INSTRUCTIONS

Prepare:

1. Wipe pots with a damp cloth to remove dust.
2. Glue pots with bottoms together.
3. Paint top 1" of candle with glass and tile medium. Let dry.
4. Basecoat pots with Light Gray. Let dry.
5. Transfer design to pots and top of candle.

Paint the Design:

1. Paint top and bottom bands, swirls, and wavy line on pots with Antique Gold.
2. Paint swirls on candle with Antique Gold. Let dry.

Finish:

1. Brush satin sealer on pots.
2. Brush sealer on painted swirls *only* on candle.
3. Put a little glue on the backs of some buttons and press on candle.
4. Snip off shanks of buttons that have them. Arrange and glue buttons on top half of pot, using photo as a guide.
5. Tie ribbon around middle where the pots were glued together.
6. Place candle in center of top pot. ❑

PALM PLANTER

By Patty Cox

Patterns on page 96

SUPPLIES

Pots:

Standard clay pot, 10-1/2"

Clay bulb pot, 8-1/2"

Paints, Mediums & Finishes:

Crackle medium

Clear acrylic spray sealer

Acrylic craft paints

> Antique White
> Burnt Sienna
> Copper
> Green Light
> Pure Black
> Raw Sienna
> Rust
> Sap Green

Tools & Other Supplies:

Paint brushes

Silicone glue

Tracing paper and pencil

Transfer paper and stylus

INSTRUCTIONS

Prepare:

Glue clay pot bases together as shown. See Fig. 1.

Paint:

1. Paint pots with Rust. Brush on areas of Copper. Let dry.
2. Apply crackle medium according to manufacturer's instructions. Let dry.
3. Topcoat with Antique White. (Cracks will form.) Let dry.
4. Transfer pattern.
5. Paint palm with Sap Green. Highlight with Green Light. Shade with Pure Black.
6. Paint basket with Raw Sienna. Shade with Burnt Sienna. Let dry.

Finish:

Spray with clear acrylic finish. ❏

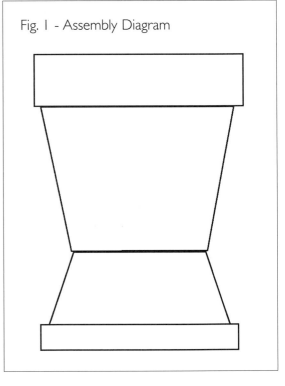

Fig. 1 - Assembly Diagram

Palm Planter
Pattern
(Actual Size)

See page 94 for instructions.

See page 98 for instructions.

MOSAIC RIMMED POT

By Holly Buttimer

A simple random mosaic of sea glass, shells, and pebbles decorates the wide rim of this pot.

Pattern on page 97

SUPPLIES

Pot:

Tall clay pot with wide rim, 8"

Paints & Finishes:

Acrylic craft paints

> Black
> Burgundy
> Deep Green
> Lavender
> Lime
> Orange
> Pale Blue
> Red
> Slate Blue
> White
> Yellow

Clear gloss acrylic sealer

Tools & Other Supplies:

Sea sponge

White grout

Lavender and purple sea glass

Small pebbles

Small seashells

Tracing paper and pencil

Transfer paper and stylus

Plastic putty knife

Paint brushes

INSTRUCTIONS

Base Paint & Sponge:

1. Paint pot below rim with Pale Blue. Let dry.
2. Dampen sponge. Sponge pot with Slate Blue, Lavender, and White, keeping colors distinct.
3. Rub the top edge of the pot with Lavender. Let dry.

Paint the Butterfly:

1. Paint wings with Orange and Yellow.
2. Shade with Burgundy.
3. Add details with Black and White.
4. Paint body and antennae with Black.

Paint the Daisies:

1. Paint centers with Yellow and Orange.
2. Paint petals with White.

Paint the Leaves:

1. Paint leaves with Deep Green.
2. Highlight with Lime.

Paint the Bee:

1. Paint bee's body with Yellow.
2. Shade with Orange. Highlight with White.
3. Outline body and paint head with Black.
4. Paint wings with White.
5. Add details and antennae with Black, using a liner brush.

Paint the Ladybug:

1. Paint body with Red.
2. Shade left side with Burgundy.
3. Highlight right side with Orange.
4. Outline and add spots and antennae with Black. Let dry.

Decorate Rim & Finish:

1. Use a putty knife to trowel grout on the rim. Press glass pieces, shells, and pebbles in grout. Let dry.
2. Seal with acrylic sealer. Let dry. ❏

PINK ROSES PLANTER

By Patty Cox

SUPPLIES

Pot:

Cylindrical clay pot with rim, 7"

Paints & Finishes:

Acrylic craft paints

    Black
    Gooseberry Pink
    Raspberry
    White

Clear acrylic spray sealer

Tools & Other Supplies:

Paint brushes

Sponge

Oven-bake polymer clay - white

Clear-drying multi-purpose glue

Paper towels

INSTRUCTIONS

Base Paint:

1. Paint top 2" of pot with Gooseberry Pink.
2. Basecoat lower portion of pot with White. Let dry.

Create the Pink Marble:

See the Marble Painting Worksheet on page 102.

1. Dab Raspberry and Gooseberry Pink dots over white paint. (Fig. 2) While wet, sponge and blend paint on white base. (Fig. 3)
2. Paint black veins on sponged area with a liner brush. While paint is wet, sponge over veins to soften. (Fig. 4)
3. Paint white veins on sponged area with a liner brush. While paint is wet, sponge over veins to soften. (Fig. 4) Let dry.

Make the Clay Roses:

1. Roll a 3/16" wide snake of clay about 9" long.
2. Coil one end of "snake" to begin rose. Pinch top of remaining snake length to make a scalloped edge. Continue coiling scalloped snake, forming a rose.
3. Repeat process (steps 1 and 2) to make 16 roses.
4. Bake roses according to clay manufacturer's instructions. Let cool.

Continued on page 102

continued from page 100

Paint the Roses:

Using a scruffy brush, force paint into crevices of roses, covering the petals. While paint is wet, wipe away paint from top edges of petals with a paper towel. Let dry.

Finish:

1. Glue roses around lower rim of pot. Let dry.
2. Spray with clear acrylic finish. ❏

Marble Painting Worksheet

Fig. 1 - Basecoat with White. Let dry.

Fig. 2 - Dab Raspberry and Gooseberry Pink dots over white paint.

Fig. 3 - While wet, sponge and blend paint on white base.

Fig. 4 - Paint Black and White veins on sponged area with a liner brush. While paint is wet, sponge over veins to soften.

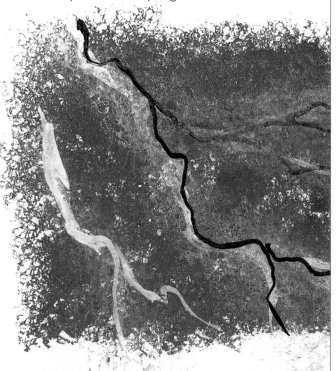

Sunflower Sundial Pattern
(Actual Size)

See page 104 for instructions.

See page 107 for additional patterns.

IV V VI VII

III

II

I

XII

XI

X

XI

X

IX VIII VII VI V

Pattern for Top

SUNFLOWER SUNDIAL

By Patty Cox

Patterns on pages 103 and 107

SUPPLIES

Pots & Saucers:

Rose clay pot, 4"

2 azalea pots, 4"

Clay saucers, 12" and 4"

Paints & Finishes:

Acrylic craft paints
  Dark Brown
  Green
  Orange
  Pine Green
  Purple
  Rust
  Yellow

Indoor/outdoor acrylic enamels
  Light Blue
  Lilac

Clear acrylic spray sealer

Paint Brushes:

Round

Flat

Liner

Tools & Other Supplies:

Expanding polyurethane foam sealant

Clear-drying multi-purpose glue

Sponge

4" plant bracket, bent at a 40 degree
  angle

Serrated edge knife

Tracing paper and pencil

Transfer paper and stylus

INSTRUCTIONS

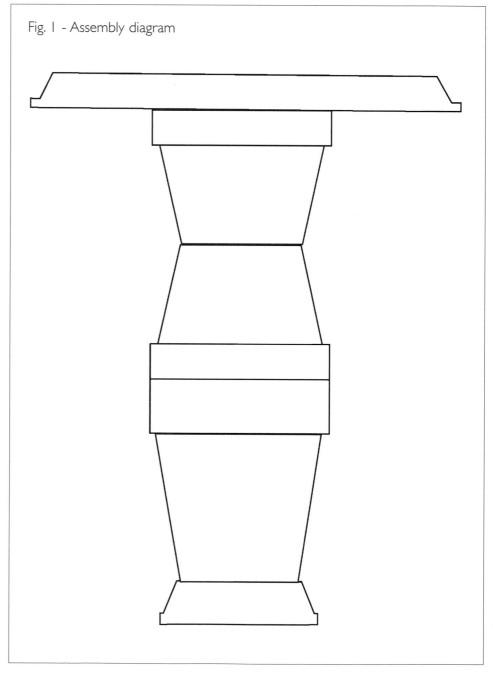

Fig. 1 - Assembly diagram

continued on page 106

continued from page 104

INSTRUCTIONS

Assemble:

See Fig. 1 on page 104.

1. Glue azalea pots together at top rims. Glue rose pot base to azalea pot base. Let dry.
2. Squirt expanding polyurethane foam inside the three pot pillar. (The foam strengthens the pot pillar.) Let dry.
3. Trim expanded foam evenly with the lips of the pots, using a serrated edge knife.
4. Glue 4" saucer to base of rose pot.

Base Paint & Sponge:

1. Paint pillar of pots and 12" saucer with Light Blue. Let dry.
2. Sponge over basecoat with Lilac. Let dry.
3. Transfer sunflower and Roman numeral patterns.
4. Glue bent plant bracket at saucer center, with the tallest point of the gnomon aligned with the number 12 (XII).

Paint the Design:

1. Double load a round brush with Yellow and Orange. Paint sunflower petals. See Example 1.
2. Load a flat brush with Yellow, Green, and Pine Green. Paint sunflower leaves. See Example 2.
3. Paint sunflower centers with Rust. Let dry. Add dark brown dots with handle end of paint brush.
4. Paint Roman numerals with Purple, using a liner brush.
5. Use the handle ends of brushes with Purple to make rows of dots between the Roman numerals and sunflower at center of saucer.

Sponge Trim:

1. Using the pattern provided, cut a triangle from the compressed sponge. Wet sponge to expand.
2. Sponge purple triangles around pillar top and bottom and along saucer sides, using photo as a guide for placement. Let dry.

Finish:

1. Glue sundial top to pillar base.
2. Spray sundial with clear acrylic finish. ❑

PAINTING EXAMPLES

Example 1 - A painted sunflower petal.

Example 2 - Flat brush loaded with Yellow, Green, and Pine Green for painting leaves.

Sponge Pattern

Sundial Planter
Patterns
(Actual Size)

Pattern for Base

Extend Stem

107

GARDEN ANGEL PLANTER

By Patty Cox

Fill the head of this stacked-pot angel with birdseed and use it as a birdfeeder, or place a pot of trailing ivy inside to give the angel a whimsical hairdo.

SUPPLIES

Pots:

Rose clay pot, 4"

Standard clay pots, two 3", 1-3/4", 4"

2 clay saucers, 4"

Paints, Mediums & Finishes:

Acrylic craft paints
> Georgia Clay
> Green Dark
> Green Light
> Green Medium
> Raw Sienna
> Sap Green
> White

Floating medium

Clear acrylic spray sealer

Tools & Other Supplies:

2 long handled teaspoons

Expanding polyurethane foam sealant

Clear-drying multi-purpose glue

Paint brushes

Spring clothespins

Serrated knife

Metal doll wings

Tape measure

Tracing paper and pencil

Transfer paper and stylus

INSTRUCTIONS

Assemble:

Refer to Figures 1 and 2 on page 110.

1. Bend "elbows" of teaspoons at a 100 degree angle, about 2-1/2" from bowl of spoon. Bend handle ends at a 30 degree angle, 1" from end. Glue bent ends inside top of azalea pot. (Fig. 1) Hold in place with spring clothespins until dry.
2. Glue azalea pots together at bases. Glue rose pot to lower azalea pot at rims. (Fig. 2) Let dry.
3. Spray polyurethane foam in the three glued pots to secure and strengthen the pillar. Spray foam in one 4" saucer. Let dry.
4. Trim expanded foam evenly with pot and saucer rims, using a serrated knife.
5. Glue 4" saucer over the top of the azalea pot at angel's "shoulders". (Fig. 2)
6. Glue the 1-3/4" pot (the angel's neck) to the base of the 3" standard pot (the angel's head). Let dry.

Transfer the Patterns:

1. Use a tape measure to measure and divide perimeter of pillar into eight sections. Pencil vertical lines around pillar to aid pattern placement.
2. Trace leaf and vein pattern and transfer to pillar.
3. Trace and transfer face pattern to "head" pot.

Paint the Face & Arms:

1. Paint eyes with White.
2. Paint irises with Green Medium. Paint pupils with Green Dark. Dot a White highlight in each pupil.
3. Outline eyes and features with Georgia Clay. Float Georgia Clay + floating medium on cheeks and eyelids. Paint lips with Georgia Clay.
4. Basecoat teaspoon arms with Georgia Clay.
5. Sponge with Raw Sienna.

Paint the Leaves & Wings:

1. Paint four center leaves on middle body with Green Light. Float veins with Green Medium.
2. Paint remaining four leaves on middle body with Green Dark. Float veins with Sap Green.

Continued on page 110

continued from page 108

3. Paint wings and remaining leaves on body with Green Medium. Float veins with Green Dark.
4. Float edges of wings with Green Dark.
5. Paint rim of neck pot with Green Dark. Let dry.

Complete Assembly & Finish:
1. Glue neck and head on top of shoulders.
2. Glue 4" saucer to base of pillar.
3. Glue wings at shoulder back.
4. Spray with clear acrylic coating. ❑

Fig. 1 - The pieces for the top half.

Fig. 2 - Assembly diagram

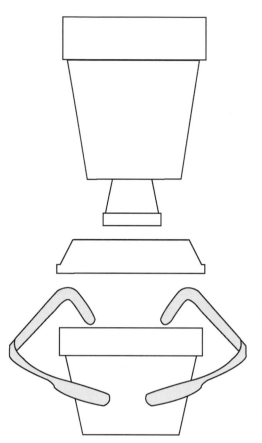

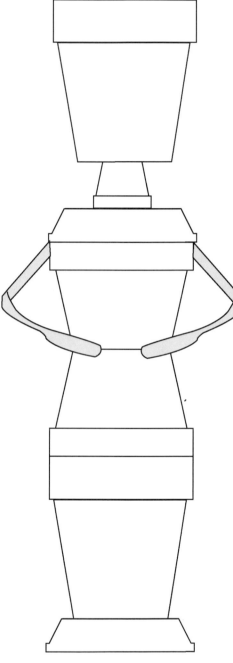

Pattern for Face
(Actual Size)

Pattern for Leaf Design
(at right)
Enlarge @125% for actual size.

Center front

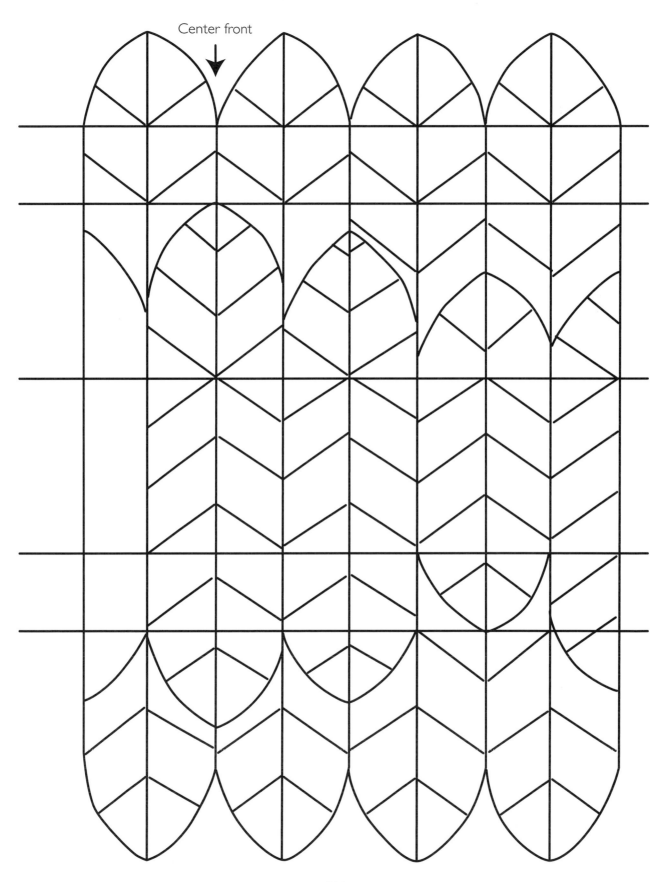

COVERED BIRDFEEDER

By Patty Cox

An upside-down metal bowl forms an umbrella over a stacked pot base and a saucer that can be filled with birdseed to create a birdfeeder.

SUPPLIES

Pots & Saucer:

2 standard clay pots, 8-1/2"

Clay saucer, 10-3/4"

Paints, Mediums & Finishes:

Indoor/outdoor gloss acrylic paint -
    Chamois

Acrylic craft paint
    Black Forest
    Olive Green

Spray paint - Rust

Crackle medium

Brush-on waterbase finish

Acrylic stain - Oak

Clear acrylic spray sealer

Brushes:

#10 flat

Sponge brushes

Tools & Other Supplies:

12" metal bowl

1 threaded rod, 24" x 5/16"

1 cap nut, 5/16"

4 washers, 5/16"

4 coupler nuts, 5/16"

Drill and 5/16" metal and masonry
    drill bits

Expanding polyurethane foam sealant

Clear-drying multi-purpose glue

Measuring tape   Pencil

Dry cloth   Bird seed

INSTRUCTIONS

Drill & Spray Paint:

1. Drill a 5/16" hole in the center of saucer, using a masonry bit.
2. Drill a 5/16" hole in the center of bowl, using a metal bit.
3. Spray paint threaded rod and inside of bowl with Rust. Let dry.

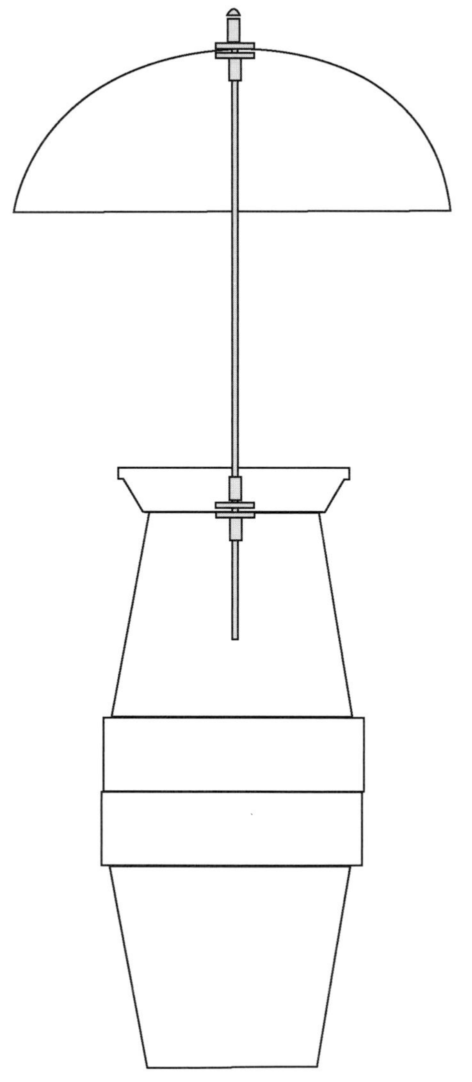

Assemble:

1. Assemble threaded rod through pot, saucer, and bowl as shown in Fig. 1. Add fender washers. Tighten coupler nuts securely.
2. Glue rim edges of clay pots together. Let dry.
3. Spray polyurethane foam sealant through bottom holes of pots. Allow to dry and cure eight hours.

Paint:

1. Base paint clay pots with Chamois, leaving inside of saucer unpainted. Let dry.
2. Divide circumference of pots into eight sections. Pencil vertical lines at each mark. Divide bowl "umbrella" into eight sections. Pencil vertical lines at each mark. (These lines will be the fern stems.)
3. Mark 1" increments along vertical lines. Pencil frond lines pointing at 45 degree angles from stem. *Note:* The fronds on the base point upward. The fronds on the bowl point downward. See painting diagram on page 115.

continued on page 114

Fig. 1 - Assembly Diagram

continued from page 112

4. Double load a #10 flat brush with Olive Green and Black Forest. Place brush on penciled center stem line. Wiggle brush back and forth to paint a frond, ending each with a point. See the Painting Example below. Repeat to paint remaining fronds.
5. To paint the center stem, double load a #10 flat brush with Olive Green and Black Forest. Paint a narrow dash between each frond. Let dry.

Crackle & Stain :
1. Apply crackle medium over painted surfaces. Let dry.
2. Brush with waterbase varnish. Cracks will form.
3. Brush stain over surface with a sponge brush, making horizontal strokes. Wipe away with a dry cloth, allowing stain to settle in the cracks. Let dry.

Finish:
1. Spray with clear acrylic coating. Let dry.
2. Fill saucer with bird seed. ❑

PAINTING EXAMPLE

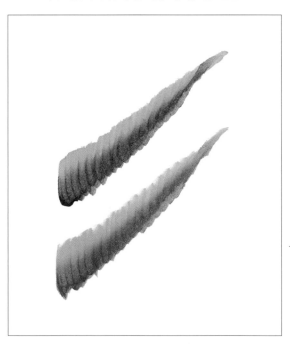

Covered Birdfeeder Painting Diagram

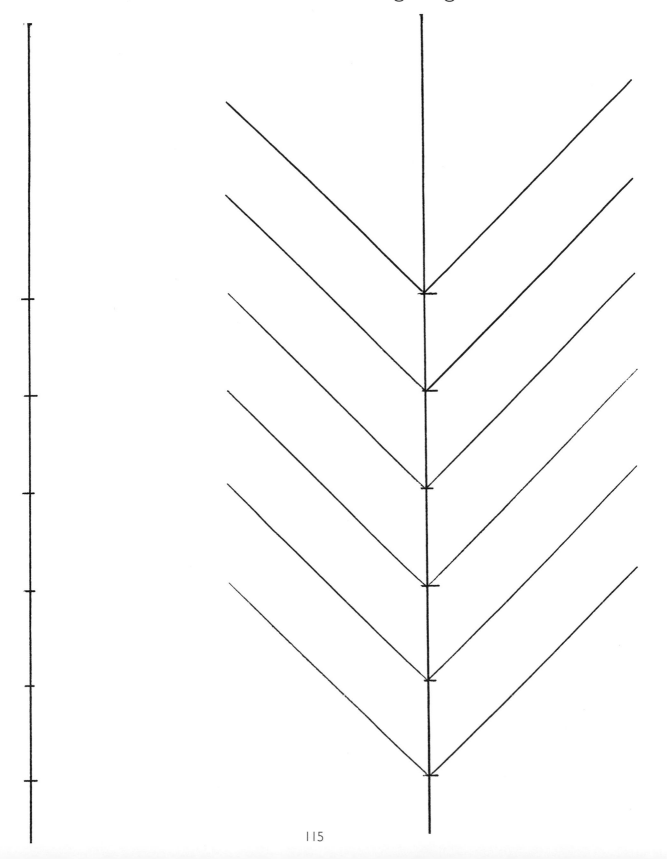

GINGERBREAD
COOKIE
JAR

By Karen Embry

A pot covered with an upside-down saucer makes a great cookie jar. Gel molding paste is mixed with white craft paint and applied with a craft tip to create the dimensional decorations.

Instructions follow on page 118.

SUPPLIES

Pot & Saucer:

Clay azalea pot, 8-1/4"

Clay saucer

Paints & Finishes:

Acrylic craft paints
   Country Twill
   Nutmeg
   Parchment
   Wicker White

Matte spray sealer

Brushes:

Wash, 1"

Tools & Other Supplies:

Puffed wooden gingerbread shapes

Gel modeling paste

Craft tip set

2" wooden knob

5/8 yd. burgundy wire-edge ribbon,
   1-1/2" wide

White craft glue

Small plastic bottle

INSTRUCTIONS

Prepare & Base Paint:
1. Wipe all dust from clay pot and saucer.
2. Paint pot and saucer with Country Twill. Let dry.

Paint the Design:
1. Paint band at top of pot and wooden knob with Parchment.
2. Paint wooden gingerbread shapes with Nutmeg.
3. Mix equal amounts gel molding paste and Wicker White. Put this mixture in a small plastic bottle. Put craft tip on bottle. Use the mixture to squeeze the design on the gingerbread shapes and on the lid and to add the lettering on the pot. Let dry.

Finish:
1. Glue wood knob on top of clay saucer.
2. Glue gingerbread men around rim of clay pot. Let dry.
3. Apply two coats of matte sealer spray. Let dry.
4. Tie ribbon to wood knob. ❑

Gingerbread Cookie Jar Pattern
(Actual Size)

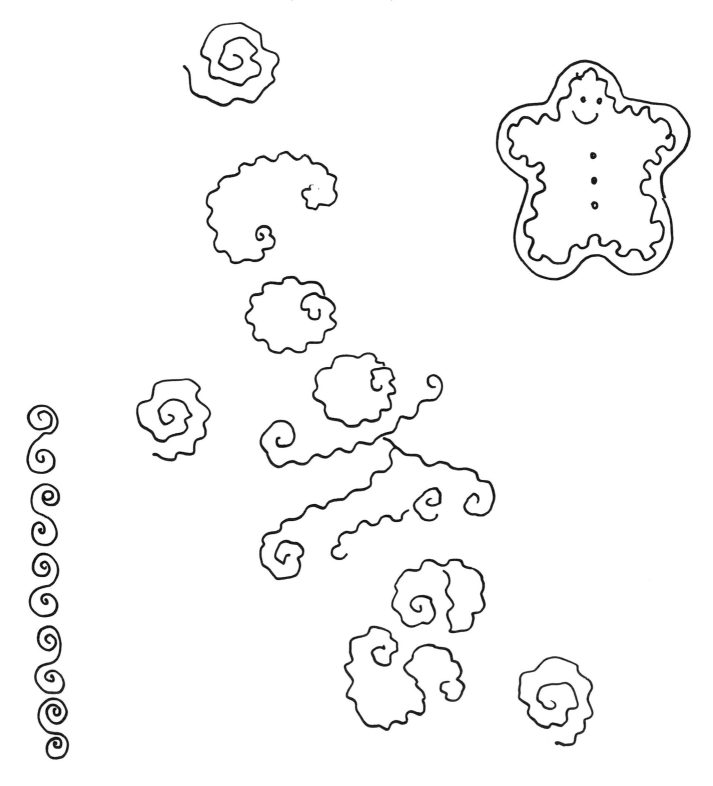

SNOW FAIRY

By Karen Embry

SUPPLIES

Pots & Saucer:

2 standard clay pots, 3"

1 clay saucer

Paints & Finishes:

Acrylic craft paints

    Inca Gold (metallic)

    Licorice

    Magenta

    Patina

    Pink

    Pure Orange

    Titanium White

Matte spray sealer

Tools & Other Supplies:

Medium round-top wooden finial

2 mushroom plugs, 1/2"

Nylon angel wings with glitter, 3-1/4"

Scepter with star, 18mm

White craft glue

Transfer paper

Black ink pen, .05

INSTRUCTIONS

Prepare & Base Paint:

1. Wipe dust from clay pots and saucer. Glue pieces together to form body with wooden finial on top, using the photo as a guide.
2. Paint all body pieces with Titanium White. Let dry.
3. Transfer design to face and upper body.

Paint the Finial Bands:

1. Paint band just below head with Pink.
2. Paint next band with Magenta.
3. Paint bottom band with Inca Gold.

Paint the Face;

1. Base nose with Pure Orange.
2. Base pupils with Patina.
3. Paint lips and heart on body with Magenta.
4. Slightly rub in a small amount of Pink in cheek area.

Paint the Base:

1. Paint bottom band on rim of clay saucer with Magenta.
2. Paint next band on rim with Pink.
3. Paint bottom of saucer with Inca Gold.
4. Add Titanium White dots on the Magenta band.

Finish:

1. Add line work with the ink pen. Let dry.
2. Spray with a light coat of matte sealer, misting lightly so ink won't run. Let dry.
3. Glue on hands (the mushroom plugs), wand, and wings, using the photo as a guide for placement. ❏

Pattern for Face
(actual size)

TERRA COTTA TIERS FOUNTAIN

by Patty Cox

Simple and inexpensive terra cotta pots and saucers of varying sizes make exceptionally nice fountains. They are very easy to assemble and maintain. And your imagination is the limit when it comes to size. Just as long the proportion of the saucers and pots works, then your fountain can be tiny — made with 2" and 3" pots; or larger — made with 6" and 8" pots with appropriate sized saucers. When making a larger fountain, be sure to buy a pump that will push the water high enough for your size fountain. Mossy plants or fern work well in this fountain.

SUPPLIES

Pump: Outdoor submersible water pump or fountain pump

Tubing: Clear plastic 3/8" tubing

Design Feature: Two clay pots, 4" and 3"

Container: Three clay saucers, 11", 8" and 4"; Three clay planter feet (Fig. 1)

Filler: River stones

Sealants: Flexible industrial strength glue; silicone caulking; Epoxy resin finish

Tools: Mini drill and silicone carbide grinding stone bit

INSTRUCTIONS

Refer to Figures 1 - 3 on page 124.

1. Waterproof the inside of the largest terra cotta saucer with epoxy resin. Allow to dry and cure. This is the only one that needs to be water-tight.

2. Ream out the holes in the bottom of the 4" and 3" pots, if needed, to 3/8" diameter so that tubing can go through the holes. Use a mini drill with grinding stone bit.

3. Drill 3/8" holes in centers of 4" and 8" saucers to accommodate tubing.

4. The 4" pot at the bottom is the pump housing. Turn it upside down and glue the 8" saucer centered on top, aligning holes. Glue the 4" saucer on top of inverted 3" pot, aligning holes. See Fig. 2

5. Push the plastic tubing through the 4" pot and saucer, then through the 3" pot and saucer. Trim tubing evenly with surface on top of 4" saucer. See Fig. 3. Use silicone caulking around the hole in the top saucer to seal the hole and to secure the tubing.

6. Place the pump in the 11" saucer as shown in Fig. 3. Secure tubing on pump's outflow post, trimming length of tubing as needed.

7. Place the housing pot (4" pot) over the pump on the terra cotta feet.

8. Add water to the 11" saucer. Adjust water flow speed.

9. Fill all three saucers with river stones. ❏

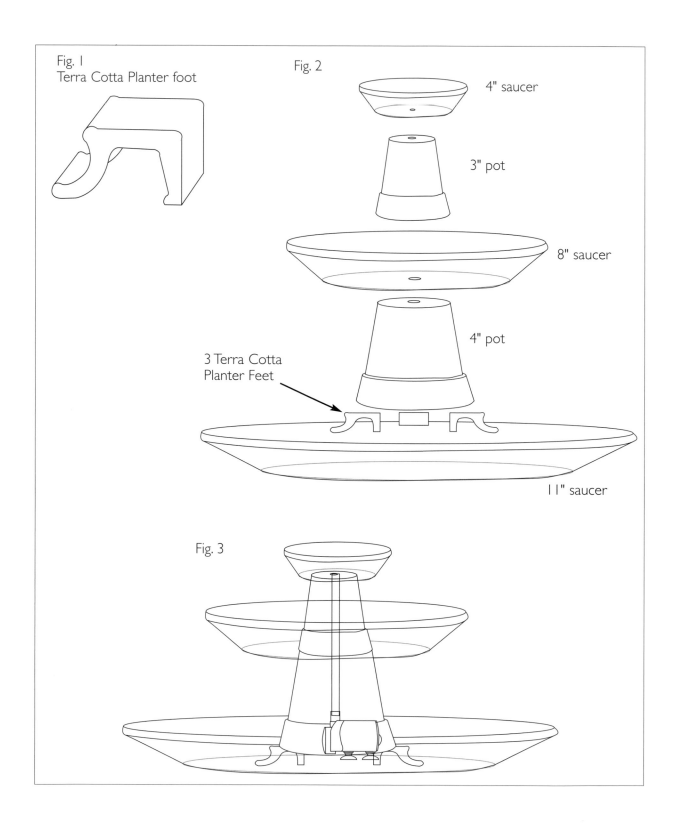

Fig. I
Terra Cotta Planter foot

Fig. 2

4" saucer

3" pot

8" saucer

4" pot

3 Terra Cotta
Planter Feet

11" saucer

Fig. 3

METRIC CONVERSION CHART

Inches to Millimeters and Centimeters

Inches	MM	CM
1/8	3	.3
1/4	6	.6
3/8	10	1.0
1/2	13	1.3
5/8	16	1.6
3/4	19	1.9
7/8	22	2.2
1	25	2.5
1-1/4	32	3.2
1-1/2	38	3.8
1-3/4	44	4.4
2	51	5.1
3	76	7.6
4	102	10.2
5	127	12.7
6	152	15.2
7	178	17.8
8	203	20.3
9	229	22.9
10	254	25.4
11	279	27.9
12	305	30.5

Yards to Meters

Yards	Meters
1/8	.11
1/4	.23
3/8	.34
1/2	.46
5/8	.57
3/4	.69
7/8	.80
1	.91
2	1.83
3	2.74
4	3.66
5	4.57
6	5.49
7	6.40
8	7.32
9	8.23
10	9.14

INDEX

INDEX